WORKSHOP MODELS FOR FAMILY LIFE EDUCATION

FOUR ONE-DAY WORKSHOPS

Kathyryn Apgar and Betsy Nicholson Callahan

RCI Resource Communications Inc.
1616 Soldiers Field Road, Boston, Massachusetts 02135

Published by RCI in cooperation with Family Service Association of America

ACKNOWLEDGMENTS

Editors: Anne S. Glickman and Nancy Witting; Proofreader: Linda Lord; Typesetting and layout: Nancy L. Weston.

Library of Congress Cataloging in Publication Data

Apgar, Kathryn.
　　　Four one-day workshops.

　　　(Workshop models for family life education)
　　　"Published by RCI in cooperation with Family
Service Association of America."
　　　Bibliography: p. 6.
　　　1. Family life education—handbooks, manuals,
etc. I. Callahan, Betsy Nicholson, 1947—joint author.
II. Family Service Association of America. III. Title.
IV. Series.
HQ10.A64　　　　306.8　　　　80.5952
ISBN 0-86618-004-4

PREFACE

Family Life Education (FLE) is a social work method utilizing adult education techniques. It is a group method for assisting individuals, couples and families in broadening their knowledge of behavioral alternatives available for coping more effectively with the developmental stages of life and with situational crises. The major objectives of FLE are to increase knowledge, change attitudes and increase behavioral skills. Its theoretical base includes theories of learning, communication, crisis, systems and adult education. FLE is now a growing form of practice in family and children's services and in community mental health programs. This reflects renewed interest in preventative programs which build on the strengths of people, not as clients, but as community members.

This model was developed out of many years of experience by the staff of the Family Life Education Program at the Family Service Association of Greater Boston. Family Service has a long history of providing Family Life Education, and their staff is recognized nationally as leaders in this field.

The author(s) encourage the creative and flexible use of this model. It is intended as a guide. You are encouraged to adapt it to suit your own teaching style and to meet the needs of your particular group.

–Donald P. Riley
Director of Professional and
Community Development
Family Service Association of
Greater Boston

CONTENTS

1   INTRODUCTION

9   SELF-ESTEEM DAY FOR WOMEN

37   ASSERTIVENESS TRAINING

65   CREATIVE CONTACT FOR SINGLES

87   STRESS MANAGEMENT

INTRODUCTION

These one-day workshops were developed for people who cannot commit the time to participate in workshop meetings for a period of 6 to 8 weeks. Some people come to test out their interest in developing increased self-awareness and new skills, or to assess their comfort with a group approach to personal issues. For some individuals, a good workshop experience can lead to a commitment to personal growth carried out individually or with professional guidance.

Necessarily, less material is covered during a one-day workshop than during a series of meetings. However, although content is reduced, the benefits of a group experience are greatly enhanced. Attractive features for leaders are freedom from the problems associated with absentees, such as lack of participant continuity, and the need for follow-up communication.

The one-day format provides the equivalent of three two-hour workshops, scheduled as a six-hour day. A number of structural elements contribute to cohesion and group support. One-day formats generate a high level of energy, participation, and optimism. Because of the extended time spent together, people get to know each other better and more quickly. Lunch can be shared formally or informally as a whole group or in small groups as people wish. It is not uncommon for friendships to develop and support networks to evolve. A real sense of progress is expressed, and a visible shift is observed from feelings of uncertainty and self-doubt at the beginning to an upbeat positive attitude and willingness to try out new skills at the end of the day.

AUDIENCE

The audiences you will be reaching are women for Self-Esteem Day; and both men and women for Assertiveness Training, Stress Management, and Creative Contact for Singles. The singles groups will include never-marrieds, people who are separated or divorced, and widows and widowers. If you wish to include working men and women, we suggest you consider scheduling meetings on weekends; we have been successful in attracting participants on Saturdays between 9:30 a.m. and 4:00 p.m.

You should decide what the enrollments will be. We recommend no fewer than 15 people. If the workshop will have over 25 people, it is helpful to have two leaders.

PROMOTING THE GROUP

Work with a Cosponsor

Cosponsoring the program with another well-known and respected organization in the community that works with adults can greatly help in the recruitment of group members.

Flyers

Having a brief, attractive, eye-catching flyer is an effective way to promote the workshop. If you work in a human services organization, send a flyer to all members of the staff with a brief cover memo, and ask them to review their client lists and let you know of people they think would benefit from the group. Also, contact any organizations or facilities in the area that come into contact with the population you hope to attract, and send flyers to them for distribution.

Mailings

We have found that a direct mailing of flyers about one month prior to the workshop is the most effective way to recruit participants. You may want to include a tear-off form for applicants to mail in. This form should include the applicant's address and phone number. You may also wish to follow up the mailing with a phone call. Frequently, potential participants do not apply formally for the workshop but respond positively to a telephone call.

Use of Publicity

Make use of your community's free publicity sources. Radio stations, newspapers, and television stations offer free public service announcements. A brief description of the workshop (dates, place, and so on) and dates to air the announcement should be sent to the public service director of the media chosen. Contact local stations and newspapers for the format each requires for such announcements and for deadline dates. Note, too, that some newspapers may be willing to print a short article on the workshop. This provides greater visibility than a public service announcement. It is usually necessary to write a formal news release for this.

TIPS FOR ENSURING GOOD ATTENDANCE

It is a good idea to speak with every applicant on the telephone before the workshop begins. This allows participants to establish an official contact with the group leader ahead of time, to ask questions, and to iron out any difficulties that might prevent them from attending the workshop.

SUGGESTED FORMAT FOR THE DAY

Arrive at least an hour ahead of time to take care of last-minute preparations and to be present when the first person arrives. It is not unusual for someone to arrive an hour before the starting time!

Use the first half-hour for registration. Have food and beverages available during registration—donuts, pastry, coffee, tea. Instruct people about the location of the bathrooms and coatrooms. They can begin to meet others during this time. Give out name cards and have people fill them out.

It is important to build in two breaks in the morning and two in the afternoon, in addition to lunch. You might want to have beverages available at those times. People do get tired of sitting for long periods and need at least to get up, stretch, and move about.

Lunch can be provided if you have the facilities to do this, or participants can bring lunch and you provide beverages. We recommend that participants have lunch together, which becomes part of the workshop experience. If this is not realistically possible for you, and people will have to go out for lunch, you will have to allow at least an hour.

Morning sessions begin with registration between 9:30 and 10:00; the workshop content begins at 10:00, continuing to 12:30; lunch break is about 45 minutes, and the afternoon session is about 2½ hours in length, ending at 4:00 p.m.

AGENDA

An agenda is provided for each session. You can display this on a flip-chart or chalkboard and go over it at the start of the workshop. This lets the group know what is to be covered that day. You should fill in the time for each section of the workshop after deciding what you will be covering and estimating how long each activity should run.

3

MATERIALS

All materials used in the workshop are relatively inexpensive and readily available. You will need:

    flipchart or chalkboard
    pencils
    felt markers or chalk and eraser
    5 x 8" unlined cards for name tags
    safety pins or masking tape
    copies of the handouts
    lunches if you plan to provide them
    beverages and food for breaks.

NAME TAGS

Before the workshop, prepare 5 x 8" name tags by drawing a large triangle on each with a marker or crayon. Have felt markers or crayons available for participants to use for filling in. Provide masking tape or safety pins so that participants can attach their name tags to their clothing.

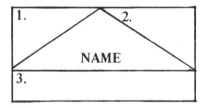

When participants arrive, instruct them to print their first names in large letters inside the triangle. Then ask them to fill in the rest of their name tag according to the instructions provided for each workshop. These instructions should be written where everyone can see them.

HANDOUTS

Handouts accompany each workshop and need to be duplicated ahead of time. Read the workshop guide carefully to determine if handouts are to be used during the session or given out at the end.

LEADER'S PREPARATION

Most important, read the workshop guide very carefully and plan out how to handle each portion of the workshop. You should be familiar enough

4

with the content, activities, and the materials needed that you do not have to consult the guide at every moment. The more spontaneous your presentation is, and the more responsive you are to the audience, the more effective the workshop will be.

Mini-lectures
The manual provides basic information for each mini-lecture. Present mini-lectures in your own words, modifying them to suit your style and your group. You will be most effective if you adapt the mini-lecture to fit the group's learning needs, expectations, and past learning experiences. You may decide to spend more time on one section than another, adding your own material or modifications. Be creative!

For example, as noted in the manual, some mini-lectures may be most effective when presented directly by you, while others may serve mainly as background, with open discussion being the primary means of covering the material.

You may want to practice presenting some of the material ahead of time.

A simple and informal way to present mini-lecture material is to list key ideas on a flipchart or chalkboard ahead of time. This list serves as a guide for your talk. Also, groups tend to respond more positively when mini-lectures include such visual aids.

We recommend that you limit lectures to 15 minutes to allow time for exercises and discussion. From our experience, participants learn more from active involvement than from simply listening to presentations.

Coleaders
If two of you will be leading the workshop, plan ahead of time who will do what. We recommend that you alternate presentations of content and exercises. This approach is stimulating for the group, because of your different styles. Each of you will be sharing responsibility for presenting content, leading discussions, and conducting exercises. While one is talking, the other can be noting participants' responses to the material and activities, and observing group process issues. We suggest you limit the lecture time to not over 15 minutes to allow more time for exercises and discussion. In our experience, all participants enjoy and learn more from active involvement than from extended periods of passive listening.

LEADER'S ROLE

You will be filling many roles—facilitator, resource person, teacher. A knowledge of group processes, adult learning theory, and human growth and development will contribute to your success in conducting workshops. If you are a beginner in this field, you might consider locating someone in the human services profession with experience in leading educational workshops who could offer guidance. Training in adult education/family life education is available through universities and Family Service Associations.

Beginning leaders may wish to adhere closely to the original model, while more experienced leaders may decide to use sections of the material selectively. We encourage you to be creative and flexible in using the models, and to adapt them to your own teaching style.

SUGGESTED READINGS

For leaders who have no background relating to each of the workshops, we recommend the following books. You may want to search out other pertinent articles or books. By reading in each area ahead of time, you will be able to enrich the quality of your presentations and group discussions.

Self-Esteem

Jongeward, Dorothy and Scott, Dru. *Women as Winners.* Reading, Mass.: Addison-Wesley, 1976. Contains exercises and techniques to change your life in a positive way. Read about how many women live like fairy-tale characters—Cinderella, Sleeping Beauty, etc.

Porat, Frieda. *Positive Selfishness.* Millbrae, Calif.: Celestial Arts, 1977. A practical guide to building positive self-esteem with exercises and discussion of components of self-esteem.

Zimbardo, Philip G. *Shyness, What It Is, What To Do About It.* Reading, Mass.: Addison-Wesley, 1977. A psychologist discusses why people are shy and presents some effective techniques used at his Stanford University Shyness Clinic to cope with this problem.

Assertiveness Training

Alberti, Dr. Robert and Emmons, Michael. *Your Perfect Right: A Guide to Assertive Behavior.* San Luis Obispo, Calif.: Impact, Box 1094, 1974.

Bloom, Dr. Lynn; Coburn, Karen; and Pearlman, Joan. *The New Assertive Woman.* New York: Dell Publishing Company, 1975. A readable, comprehensive guide for men and women.

Fensterheim, Dr. Herbert and Baer, Jean. *Don't Say Yes When You Want to Say No.* New York: Dell Publishing Company, 1975. Contains numerous vignettes to help you learn how to apply assertive communication in close personal relationships, on the job, and in social situations.

Smith, Dr. Manuel. *When I Say No I Feel Guilty.* New York: Bantam Books, 1975.

So many new books on assertiveness training come out periodically that we have only listed four tried and true books. Many other excellent books on the subject are available that you may also want to read.

Being Single

Edwards, Marie and Hoover, Eleanor. *The Challenge of Being Single.* New York: New American Library, 1974. Advice on getting the most out of being single, whether widowed, divorced, or never married. Chapter 7 discusses resources and activities for singles.

Ford, Edward E. and Zorn, Robert L. *Why Be Lonely?* Niles, Ill.: Argus Communications, 1975. How to build quality relationships following the initial chemistry phase and some ideas about where to find friends.

Stein, Peter J. *Single.* Englewood Cliffs, N.J.: Prentice-Hall, 1976. An overview of the life experiences of single men and women based on interviews with singles. Considers the trend toward growing numbers of singles in the U.S., the relationship of single adults and their parents, sexual issues, and the potential for singlehood as a social movement.

Stress

Ardell, Donald B. *High Level Wellness: An Alternative to Doctors, Drugs, and Disease.* New York: Bantam Books, 1977, 1979. Gives an overview of a variety of stress reduction approaches and includes a discussion of nutrition and physical fitness.

Benson, Herbert, M.D. *The Relaxation Response.* New York: Morrow, 1975. Complete instructions for practicing the relaxation response. Dr. Benson presents the universal principles underlying all relaxation and meditation methods that he incorporated into the method he developed.

Friedman, Meyer, M.D. and Rosenman, Ray H., M.D. *Type A Behavior and Your Heart.* New York: Fawcett Crest Books, 1974. The authors describe some helpful approaches for changing Type A behaviors.

Selye, Hans, M.D. *The Stress of Life.* Rev. Ed. New York: McGraw-Hill, 1978. The pioneer researcher in this field describes both the physiological mechanisms that are actuated when we experience stress and a philosophical approach to managing stress.

SELF-ESTEEM DAY FOR WOMEN

AGENDA

   I. INTRODUCTION: GETTING ACQUAINTED AND SETTING OBJECTIVES

  II. MINI-LECTURE AND EXERCISE: WHAT IS SELF-ESTEEM?

 III. EXERCISES: BUILDING SELF-ESTEEM

 IV. RECOGNIZING YOUR STRONG POINTS

     (Lunch)

  V. MINI-LECTURE: ACCEPTING YOURSELF

 VI. MINI-LECTURE: TAKING CHARGE OF YOUR LIFE

 VII. SUMMING UP

VIII. EVALUATION OF WORKSHOP

I. INTRODUCTION: GETTING ACQUAINTED AND SETTING OBJECTIVES

Fill Out Name Tags

Ask participants to fill out name tags as they arrive and to list brief answers to the following questions. Write questions on flipchart or chalkboard where everyone can see them.

• What is your definition of self-esteem?

• What are some of the ways in which you put yourself down?

• What do you hope to learn or accomplish today?

Introduce Yourself

Tell participants your name and give any background about your experience in leading groups and in building self-esteem.

Describe how you will be handling role of leader: that you will be structuring the activities and acting as a facilitator and resource person.

Share the following information in your own words: "Large numbers of women suffer from low self-esteem, which burdens their growth and happiness. We know that much of this devaluation of self comes from women's socialization and treatment in our society. Fortunately, self-confidence and positive feelings about oneself can be developed. We plan today to help you see where you have developed low self-esteem, and to teach you some steps to build attitudes and ways of dealing with others that will enhance your self-esteem."

Overview of Workshop

Display agenda on flipchart where everyone can see it and review it briefly so that participants have a general idea of the day's structure and activities.

Setting Objectives

"At this point I'd like you to meet one another and find out what others hope to gain from today's experience. To accomplish this with a large crowd, I use an exercise called Party Mix. Each of you filled out a name tag and answered three questions:

• What is your definition of self-esteem?

• What are some ways in which you put yourself down?

• What do you hope to learn or accomplish today?

"I'd like you to stand up. Mill around silently and read as many messages as you can while others are reading yours. When I say stop, form groups with two people you don't know, then sit down with your group. (Allow five minutes for milling, then call 'stop.')

"Now that you are in triads, please count off 1, 2, 3. Person 1 will begin by talking for one minute about any aspects of her name tag that she would like (any or all of three responses to the questions we asked). When we call time, switch to person 2. Person 2 will have one minute to talk, then on to person 3."

II. MINI-LECTURE AND EXERCISE: WHAT IS SELF-ESTEEM?

Soliciting Group Definitions
"Before we begin our mini-lecture, we'd like to hear some of your definitions of self-esteem. We'd like a volunteer from each group to summarize the three definitions from your group. We're going to list these on a flip-chart so we can all look at the basic components of self-esteem." (You may make comments during this exercise, tying the group's definitions to the material that follows. Allow 10 to 15 minutes for the exercise.)

What Is Self-Esteem?
" 'Self-esteem is an evaluation of your own worth based on how you compare yourself with others.' The end result of your evaluation will be feelings of worth or worthlessness. When making comparisons with others, people can get into trouble. It's okay to admire people who have been outstanding, but if you set their level of success as a benchmark for your own aspirations, you may end up feeling frustrated and unhappy. Suppose you want to think like Albert Einstein, write like William Faulkner, single like Carly Simon, lead the social life of Jackie Kennedy. These people are inappropriate models for comparison because they've achieved extraordinary success and recognition that few people can enjoy. You also run the risk of focusing on the status or achievement only—the end product—rather than the process of development and growth that led to success. Finally, you run the risk of trying to be like someone else, rather than developing and enjoying your own particular talents and strengths.

---

[1] Philip G. Zimbardo. *Shyness: What It Is, What To Do About It.* Reading, Mass.: Addison-Wesley, 1977, p. 154.

14

"Family, friends, work associates, community, the media—all influence a person's self-esteem. Today, we'll be presenting ideas and activities that will expand your awareness of these influences. Our goal is to help you make choices based on informed awareness of your self-image, rather than deciding what is easiest at the moment or making no decisions at all and just drifting through life."

EXERCISE

Exercise: Glass of Water[1]
"We have all heard the story of a glass being described as half-empty by pessimists and half-full by optimists.

"Let's equate self-esteem with a glass of water. The more water you have in your glass today, the more self-esteem you feel. For some people the glass is so full of water that it runs over the rim; others have no water at all in their glass. Some of you will find your glass of water today to be one-half, one-quarter, or three-quarters full.

"Some days someone knocks your glass over and all the water spills out. Some days you have a crack in your glass, and no matter how much water you pour in it just leaks out."

Draw a large glass on a flipchart, paper, or chalkboard, and ask participants to come up and draw the level of the water in their glass for today.

This is an excellent exercise for making the concept of self-esteem concrete and understandable to a group. Note briefly the group's collective level of self-esteem today. Assure them that it is usual to begin the workshop with low self-esteem and you expect everyone's self-esteem to rise by the end of the day. You may want to repeat this exercise just before the evaluation of the workshop, to measure any change that has taken place.

What Is a Person with High Self-Esteem Like?
"A person with high self-esteem projects poise, self-confidence, and optimism, which come from feeling satisfied with herself. She has learned the art of being her own best friend and biggest booster, and does not depend on the praise and encouragement of others in order to like herself. People who have high self-esteem are 'doers': They are participators, activators, facilitators. A woman who has high self-esteem doesn't feel she's worthless

---

[1] Contributed by Rick Scaramozza, Family Service Association of Greater Boston.

15

if someone says 'no' to her, or if she is handed a criticism. Instead she takes a constructive, problem-solving approach to criticism, and analyzes negative feedback she has received. This may provide useful clues to her about aspects of herself that she may want to try to change.

"On the other hand, the negative response she receives may have little or nothing to do with her; it may well be the other person's problem. In any event, she does not put herself down because of receiving a rejection. A woman with high self-esteem has learned to accept all of herself, both her minuses and pluses. She sees herself as important, competent, and capable of making her own decisions. She also can ask for help when she wants it. She allows herself to be in touch with her whole range of feelings—sadness, anger, joy, pride, love, hate. She knows what she wants, is tuned into her feelings, and accepts this total package as herself. Because she allows herself to 'own' all of her thoughts, feelings, and wishes, it becomes easier to love and care for herself and to feel she deserves to be happy. She does not torture herself with the flaws in herself or her situation; she builds on the strengths in her personality for growth. She does not delude herself that she is perfect; she accepts imperfection as part of the human condition, while working to change what can realistically be changed. Such a woman knows she has the power and responsibility to design her own life, to make it happer and more fulfilling. She takes an active approach toward life, and believes that self-acceptance and inner growth are possible for everyone. With this outlook she can give up the role of victim and take responsibility for shaping her own life."

What Is a Person with Low Self-Esteem Like?
"A person with low self-esteem lacks self-confidence, has a pessimistic outlook, is shy, and doesn't like herself much. She is overly sensitive to criticism. When she is criticized or refused something, her feeling of worhlessness increases. She depends on other people to tell her she is lovable, doing a good job, or is okay, because she does not value herself. There may be long barren periods when others don't supply her with good feelings about herself. Even when she is praised she has difficulty accepting compliments: 'You can't mean that.' 'It was nothing.' 'You're just saying that to make me feel good.' She is clearly her own worst enemy! Her approach to life is passive. She expects others to give her what she needs to make her life happy, perhaps even to make decisions for her. Because she feels inferior to others, she'll settle for crumbs or take an indirect way to get what she wants, such as whining, complaining, apologizing, suffering in silence, begging for recognition, or using feminine wiles with men (being cute, helpless,

16

stupid). Most women of our generation have been programmed by our culture to behave in these ways in relation to men. A woman with low self-esteem often rejects many of her own feelings and desires as unacceptable, and as evidence that she is a bad person. She does not allow herself to take them seriously. She may think it's wrong to say anything she fears the other person won't like to hear. The result is that the other person has no idea what she wants, guaranteeing that she won't get what she needs. This reinforces her feeling that she is undeserving.

"A woman with low self-esteem is heavily influenced by others because she does not value her own ideas and feelings or may not even think through where she stands. She is likely to be less popular than people with high self-esteem because of the gloomy outlook she projects, her dependency on others, and the burden they may feel about having to build her ego.

"Attitudes about oneself are not built into genes but are learned from a number of sources. People are taught to view themselves as possessing high or low self-esteem by their families, teachers, churches, society, and the mass media.

"Anything learned can be unlearned. The hopeful message is that it is possible to increase self-esteem no matter what your age—it is never too late. People can always learn new things, feel better about themselves, and change their lives. If you really want to work at raising your self-esteem, it can be done."

(You may want to take a 5 to 10 minute break here, before proceeding.)

III. EXERCISES: BUILDING SELF-ESTEEM

"Many people put themselves down constantly; they are their own worst enemies. Areas people often pick on are:

- intelligence
- ability to be sociable
- sexuality
- body

- talents
- skills
- spiritual life
- ability to earn money.

"I'd like each of you to spend a few minutes looking at your name tag, where you listed ways you put yourself down. Add any you left out that fit in the above categories. (Allow a few minutes for participants to do this.)

"The first step toward self-acceptance is to admit that you have negative qualities, and to see that this is natural and does not threaten your basic worth as a person. Being afraid or ashamed of your negative emotions or traits is self-destructive and nonproductive. Everyone is hostile, angry, fearful, anxious, or lonely at times. We have to accept the fact that we cannot be 'all good.' Nobody is perfect; you are being harsh and unreasonable if you demand perfection of yourself."

Exercises to Build Self-Esteem
If time allows, have participants complete the "Opposing Forces" exercise (see Handouts at the end of the workshop). Give examples of how they could expand on their positive statements about themselves. Examples following "I have a lot of attractive features" might be: "Others have told me I have a lovely telephone voice." "I am a good listener." "I never forget a friend's birthday." Allow five minutes to complete the exercise. Then ask for volunteers to read one of their weaknesses and the positive statements they made in opposition. To reinforce the positive statements, you might ask people to add to each individual's positive statements. This allows participants to receive positive feedback. Suggest that in the future when they realize they are putting themselves down that they immediately think or say something positive about themselves.

Explain, with some of your own examples, the remaining exercises on the Handout sheet, "Exercises to Build Self-Esteem": "Undoing Downers" and "Shyness by Any Other Name." Tell members you will give them an exercise instruction sheet at the end of the day so they can continue a personal program at home of building self-esteem.

IV. RECOGNIZING YOUR STRONG POINTS

"The next step in accepting yourself is to affirm your positive qualities, feelings, and attributes. In order to have a loving and respecting attitude about yourself, you need to recognize your accomplishments and talents. Low self-esteem develops by focusing on lacks, failures, and bad qualities.

18

High self-esteem rests on awareness and acceptance of strengths as well as weaknesses. To learn to think positively, you need to describe and share with others what you like or value about yourself."

Exercise
"List six things about yourself that are really good. If you have trouble thinking of positives, look back at your list of negative traits and try to come up with one thing in each area that you are doing positively."
(Areas: intelligence, ability to be sociable, sexuality, body, talents, skills, spiritual life, ability to earn money.)

"Now look at the first thing on your list and say to yourself, 'I must be pretty good if I have this.' Patting yourself on the back for your accomplishments is not selfish—it is a form of self-acceptance."

(Note to Leader: This may be a convenient place to break for lunch.)

V. MINI-LECTURE: ACCEPTING YOURSELF

"For this portion of the workshop we've borrowed some concepts from Transactional Analysis, or 'T.A.,' as it is called. T.A. is a way of looking at and understanding human behavior. It is easy to understand, and its concepts of 'life scripts' and 'strokes' seemed to us to be especially useful for this workshop.

"We will first talk about stroking. In T.A., a 'stroke' is defined as a unit of recognition exchanged between two people. Strokes can be given in the form of touching, smiling, waving your hand, or any act that says, 'I know you're there.'

"Examples of verbal strokes are: 'Hi! How are you?' 'You're looking great.' 'I'm glad you decided to come.'

"Everyone needs to be touched and recognized by other people. Infants require actual physical contact and caressing to grow normally. In a study of hospitalized infants published in 1945, Rene Spitz found that infants who received basic physical care but were given no additional attention did not develop physically or mentally as they should; some did not survive.

"As children grow older their need for verbal recognition increases and replaces some of the need for physical contact. Psychologists have concluded that recognition is a basic human need, as crucial for growth as food, water, and air.

"In T.A., positive strokes are called 'arm fuzzies' and negative strokes 'cold pricklies.' Insincere or phony praise is termed a 'plastic fuzzy.'[1]

"Positive strokes are: direct, relevant, and appropriate; both giver and receiver feel good after stroking; the woman who is given a positive stroke feels alive, important, and intelligent. Her well-being is enhanced, the experience is nourishing to her self-esteem, and her potential to be a winner expands.

"There are two kinds of positive strokes:

- Unconditional: just for being. For example, 'I'm glad you're here.'
- Conditional: for doing. For example, 'You really saved the day for me by babysitting.'

"Positive strokes can express affectionate or appreciative feelings: 'I'm glad you're my son.' 'You know, I really enjoy working with you.'

"Sometimes they express compliments: 'That was a well-written report you submitted.' 'You did a superb job preparing dinner tonight.' Such feedback gives you information about your skills and competencies.

"One of the best ways you can give a positive stroke to another is by listening carefully when another person talks and focusing your full attention on him or her.

"People who don't receive enough positive strokes may provoke a few negative strokes. Examples of common behaviors that provoke others to give us negative strokes are: being bratty, flirting, drinking, fighting, committing delinquent or antisocial acts, overspending, making mistakes, creating 'accidents,' and procrastinating.

"As with the positive strokes, there are two kinds of negative strokes:

---

1 Here, you may want to tell the T.A. "Fuzzy Tale," which can be found in *Scripts People Live* by Claude Steiner. New York: Bantam Psychology Books, 1975, pp. 127-131. The tale illustrates in an unforgettable way the concept of stroking, its value for survival, and the negative costs of stroke deprivation.

20

- Unconditional: given without explanation. 'You get on my nerves.'
- Conditional: given for a reason. 'You get on my nerves when you don't listen.'

"Let's take a quick survey of the kinds of strokes you accept, positive or negative (just raise your hands). How many of you feel uncomfortable when someone pays you a compliment? How many find negative strokes easier to accept? You may realize that you were taught one or more rules about giving and receiving strokes. They could be:

- "Don't give strokes. Don't share good feelings. Don't go around saying nice things to people.
- "Don't ask for strokes for what you need.
- "Don't accept strokes unless people spontaneously give you what you want.
- "Don't reject unwanted strokes.
- "Don't give yourself strokes; modesty is the best policy.

"People who were taught any of these rules about giving and receiving strokes have learned what in T.A. is called basic training in lovelessness. Living by these rules results in positive stroke deprivation, which can result in low self-esteem and depression. Many people have varying degrees of difficulty accepting positive strokes from others and giving them to themselves. Saying good things about yourself seems immodest, improper, or even an insult to others. And when anyone says something nice, a common reaction is to reject the compliment by discounting it. If someone says you are intelligent, for example, your inner response may be, 'yes, but I'm ugly,' or you may think, 'these people don't really know me, so what they say is phony.' Your external response may be to shrug off the compliment or immediately say something complimentary in return, as if you 'owed' the person something for his or her nice words.

"Not accepting a positive stroke is like rubbing a steak on your arm: it can't possibly be nourishing. It may help you accept positive strokes if you think of enjoying them as you would savor a favorite food.

"To build self-esteem, you can look for ways to increase your sources of positive strokes. Expanding your social network and number of relationships is an excellent way to ensure it; saying more good things to yourself in your head will do it; exploring new ideas, becoming informed about a new area can be energizing and increase your ability to relate to other people. Learning to ask for what you want instead of expecting others to guess your needs—realizing, while asking, that the other person has the right to refuse—is another important way to feel better about yourself.

"A good way to increase positive feelings about yourself is to learn to accept and give love and approval to yourself. Do this by identifying your good aspects and then making conscious acts of self-praise. This is important because you need to replace your lifelong habit of thinking negatively about yourself. By consciously identifying and rewarding positive aspects of yourself, you are taking an active approach toward changing your attitude. If you make an effort at the same time to change things about yourself that you want to improve, your self-esteem will increase further and you will become able to tackle bigger challenges."

VI. MINI-LECTURE: TAKING CHARGE OF YOUR LIFE

Rationale
"There are many ways to take control of your life. Self-awareness must precede action. Knowledge of your strong and weak points helps you to accept yourself and to know what you need to work on. Now we want to heighten your awareness of how others have influenced your self-image and life decisions, and to help you consider the options you have to change your life patterns.

"When you evaluate your self-worth it's important to realize the possibility that you are living out someone else's script. If you are acting out a plan for your life written by someone else, you are unlikely to develop your potential in the ways that meet your personal needs and values. If you recognize you are doing this, you might consider discarding or modifying that plan. Otherwise, you risk going through life following the old blueprint, regardless of how outdated or inappropriate it is for you now.

"Scripts are written by a variety of people, known and unknown. All of us share certain scripts learned from our culture: men can't cry, women can't express anger, boys must be tough and virile, girls must be tender and nurturant. When it comes to self-esteem, women have been taught by parents, teachers, and the mass media to see themselves as incomplete, inadequate, dependent. Some scripts are quite constructive, realistically based on one's potential for growth; others contain the unfinished business of one's parents, such as a father who expects his son to become the doctor he wanted to be or the unhappy mother who teaches her daughter that men don't appreciate women. These scripts tend to be destructive and do not encourage growth.

"To help you appreciate how many women blindly follow nonwinning, go-nowhere scripts, I will describe in detail several common scripts played out by women.

"As children we learned to play different parts such as heroes, heroines, villains, victims, and rescuers. Without realizing it we select a cast of supporting characters that allow us to continue the scenario as adults.

"Some common scripts after which many women pattern their lives resemble the characters in fairytales and mythology. Here are examples of scripts some women follow."[1]

You can list the characteristics of each script discussed below on a flipchart or chalkboard. See the chart of fairytale scripts following the description of "Mother Hubbard" below.

Sleeping Beauty

"She learns as a child to think of herself as a future mommy and is interested mainly in her appearance. She sleeps instead of learning, because she is going to get married, and be 'just a housewife.' This script runs out at about age 40 when her children are grown and have left home. She plays with dolls and homemaker toys, and is dicouraged or scolded for playing with boys' toys. She is preparing herself for her role as a mother. She excludes other options. As she cultivates a passive feminine appearance and apes media models, her physical, social, and academic development ceases. She is 'sleeping,' waiting for the potential husband to appear and rescue her by giving her a purpose for living: children. Her mother probably was mainly a housewife.

"Later in life, when the children are grown and have left home, she starts to feel useless, perhaps suicidal. Or she may become a runaway wife; this is becoming more common as women experience these feelings at a younger age and become aware of other options. This commonly occurs after about 10 years of marriage. This script once fulfilled many women, when

---

[1] You may wish to refer to *Women as Winners* by Dorothy Jongeward and Dru Scott, Addison-Wesley Publishing Co., Reading, Mass., 1976, where these and other fairytale scripts are described.

the life expectancy was lower. In 1900, a woman's life expectancy was less than 50 years. Now the average is 75."

How to Change the Script

- Stop waiting for rescue

- Set new goals

- Open yourself to new learning, new experiences, new people

- Learn to enjoy life regardless of age

- Clarify what you enjoy, what you do well

- Discover what skills you have or need for holding a job

- Set long-range plans

Cinderella

"She can't be happy until something or someone puts excitement into her life. There is a strong 'until' theme in her life. She won't stop living in the cinders until a fairy godmother comes along to transform her mundane life, or a man shows up who sweeps her off her feet and wants to marry her. She won't lift a finger to help herself. She sets herself up to be used by others and feels victimized. If she holds a job, it is usually at the lowest level, and she never strives for a managerial or professional position. On the job she is the drudge, imposed on by others. She complains a lot and hates her job but won't leave it, hanging on until someone comes to rescue her. However, even if she does get married she can remain stuck in a job she hates because she commits herself to men who don't meet her needs, who are unsure of themselves, and for whom she works as hard as she did for the folks at home."

How to Change the Script

- Stop marking time and living in the future

- Stop waiting for rescue

- Stop living through others

- Become your own fairy godmother

- Start living now, developing your potential

- Set realistic goals

- Ask yourself, what do I want to do with my life, whether or not I find the right man?

24

Beauty Tends Her Beast

"Beauty has a strong belief in her power to rescue men with problems. She may have learned from her mother that beastly men are incapable of giving up a drinking or drug habit or of holding a job without the direction and support of a good, caring woman. She thinks if she works hard enough he will respond to her efforts and shed his beastly nature. When the beast fails to change as she hoped, a beauty may divorce and remarry another beast—trading in one beast for another, trying to find a man more susceptible to her magic powers whom she can transform into a prince. She doesn't use her energies to develop her own talents; instead, she is likely to work at low-paying jobs to support her beast and his problems."

How to Change the Script

- Stop collecting people who have problems and rescuing those who don't want to be rescued

- Let other people run their own lives

- Seek out happy, successful men and expect to enjoy relationships with them

- Learn to enjoy life by developing your own talents and believing you deserve to be happy

- Ask yourself, what would I do if I weren't spending so much time taking care of others?

Lady Atlas

"In the Greek myth, Atlas displeased Zeus, father of the Gods, and was doomed to hold the heavens on his shoulders; he had the chance to pass on the burden to Hercules, but he took it back. A lady Atlas also carries the miseries and troubles of the world on her back and doesn't try to give them up. She lives by the philosophy, 'if you want anything done right you have to do it yourself.' As a result, she is overburdened at home and at work. At the same time she complains a lot, blames others for her miseries, plays the victim, but refuses to take steps to solve her problems."

How to Change the Script

- Stop feeling sorry for yourself and talking about your miseries

- Stop concentrating on things that went wrong, looking for someone to blame, and encouraging others to feel guilty

- Focus on problem solving

- Talk about strengths instead of weaknesses in yourself and others
- Learn to ask for and accept help
- Encourage others to feel good rather than guilty
- Learn to enjoy and take pride in your success.

Mother Hubbard

"She is devoted to the family—a supermother, a rescuer, who ignores her own needs and then feels victimized. She believes in doing things for others, being a good helper, standing behind her man, making sure no one is hungry. She structures her time to meet others' needs: cooking, entertaining, decorating, gardening, chauffeuring. She's been portrayed on TV and in magazines as having gleaming hair and floors, beautiful children, and a loving husband who comes home to a picture-book domestic scene: piping hot dinner, immaculate house, harmonious family. She works overtime at the office; when paid a compliment she feels guiltily embarrassed and says, 'It wasn't anything.' She never feels she is good enough. She needs to keep a perfect house and be a perfect employee. She gives and gives, sacrificing her own needs and building up resentment."

How to Change the Script

- Stop acting like Supermother and feeling good only when giving
- Stop assuming others can't get along without you
- Start sharing parenting responsibilities
- Feel good about independence in others
- Take care of your health
- Listen to others
- Ask yourself, what am I good at besides mothering? What do I want and how can I ask for what I want? How can I encourage others to take responsibility for their own welfare?

26

INFORMATION TO PUT ON FLIPCHART

SLEEPING BEAUTY

a future mother solely
emphasizes appearance
devalues learning
wants to get married and be "just a housewife"
waits for rescue by husband

CINDERELLA

won't be happy until she is rescued by fairy godmother or gets married
does the dirty work
plays victim
passive
doesn't help herself

BEAUTY

a rescuer of beasts (alcoholics, school dropouts, perpetual students, gamblers,
        guys with problems)
long-suffering
undeveloped talents
doesn't believe she deserves better

LADY ATLAS

overburdened
feels sorry for herself
blames others

MOTHER HUBBARD

supermother
rescuer—feels victimized, needs to be perfect
self-sacrificing

Exercise
Have participants answer the following questions on cards. Allow 5-10 minutes before moving on to the group exercise below.

- With which script do you identify most and why?

- Do you identify with parts of more than one script?

- What role do you play? Do you play more than one role?

- Are these roles the way you want to live your life? If not, what can you do to change or free yourself from these roles?

"Scripts can be changed. To begin, you need to become aware of the blueprint you brought with you from childhood. As an adult you have options you did not have as a child; you can decide to change your life in positive ways, and rewrite the old script to suit your needs and develop the kind of life you want for yourself."

Group Exercise
Solicit from group members the ideas they came up with to change their scripts. For example, ask a "Cinderella" to share with the group her ideas for counteracting that script. Put ideas on flipchart or chalkboard.

(Note to Leader: You may want to take a short break here.)

VII. SUMMING UP

"Today we have been talking about how to establish the roots of positive self-esteem. The process involves three steps. 1) *Being aware of yourself.* We did this by looking at how we put ourselves down and then by identifying our positive qualities. Knowing yourself is built on this total awareness of your being. 2) *Accepting ourselves the way we are.* We realize we can change in positive directions and like ourselves more and more. Being able to accept and to give positive strokes and being aware of our life scripts are further aids to building healthy self-esteem. 3) *Accepting positive self-esteem.* You alone are responsible for your happiness, and therefore you must learn to make decisions and assert yourself.

"We have some handouts for you that outline steps you can take from here to build and strengthen your self-esteem. We hope that all of you will make the decision to pursue life actively, think positively of yourself, and set meaningful goals. You are the creator of your own happiness and control the direction of your life. Accept the challenge and you will find that life becomes richer day by day."

You might suggest some follow-up activities in your community that are designed to build confidence and esteem. Also, you might recommend books or articles to read. Two books we found stimulating are *Peoplemaking* by Virginia Satir (Palo Alto, Calif.: Science and Behavior Books, 1972), especially "My Declaration of Self-esteem," pp. 27-29; and *Positive Selfishness* by Frieda Porat (Millbrae, Calif.: Celestial Arts, 1977), which lists 10 roots to building self-esteem and includes numerous self-help activities.

Finally, you may wish to repeat the "Glass of Water" exercise before asking participants to evaluate the workshop.

VIII. EVALUATION OF WORKSHOP

Put the following questions on a flipchart or chalkboard:

• What is your assessment of the workshop and what are your suggestions for improving it?

• How would you comment on the style and effectiveness of the leaders?

• What did you learn about yourself or others today?

Have participants answer questions on 3 x 5" cards and hand them in. You might ask them to leave their name tags so that you will have a record of people's goals; these may help you plan future workshops.

HANDOUTS FOR

SELF-ESTEEM DAY FOR WOMEN

EXERCISES TO BUILD SELF-ESTEEM[1]

Undoing Downers

Keep track of what triggers negative self-statements in you for two weeks (chart them). What seems to happen over and over that causes you to put yourself down?

Become actively conscious of your negative self-talk. Every time you start to put yourself down, say, "Stop." Practice this until you stop putting yourself down all the time.

Keep a chart of how many times a day you can keep yourself from thinking these negative thoughts. Reward yourself for suppressing them.

Opposing Forces

Make a list of your weaknesses. Put them on the left side of the page. Then, put the opposite positive statements on the right side. For example:

Weakness	Opposition
No one who knows me likes me.	Everyone who really knows me likes me.
There are few things about me that are attractive.	I have a lot of attractive features.

Expand on your statements in the "Opposition" column. Give examples. Begin to think of yourself in terms of the right-hand column instead of the left-hand one.

Shyness by Any Other Name

Many times we are shy in only one or two situations, yet we think and speak of ourselves as shy people.

Instead of thinking and saying, "I am a shy person," start thinking and talking about yourself in more specific terms; describe specific situations and specific reactions. Say, "I get nervous when I have to talk to groups," or "Parties make me feel out of place and cause me to feel weak inside," or "I feel anxious around the president of our company." Or, even more specifically, "My heart starts to pound and I get butterflies in my stomach when I know a man is checking me out."

Make as complete a list as you can of these situation-specific reactions. Then, plan what you have to do to control and change that reaction.

---

[1] Reprinted from *Shyness: What It Is, What To Do About It* by Philip G. Zimbardo, copyright 1977, by permission of Addison-Wesley Publishing Co., Reading, Mass.

FIFTEEN STEPS TO A MORE CONFIDENT YOU[1]

1. Recognize your strengths and weaknesses and set your goals accordingly.

2. Decide what you value, what you believe in, what you realistically would like your life to be like. Take inventory of your library of stored scripts and bring them up-to-date, in line with the psychological space you are in now, so they will serve you where you are headed.

3. Determine what your roots are. By examining your past, seek out the lines of continuity and the decisions that have brought you to your present place. Try to understand and forgive those who have hurt you and not helped when they could have. Forgive yourself for mistakes, sins, failures, and past embarrassments. Permanently bury all negative self-remembrances after you have sifted out any constructive value they may provide. The bad past lives on in your memory only as long as you let it be a tenant. Prepare an eviction notice immediately. Give the room to memories of your past successes, however minor.

4. Guilt and shame have limited personal value in shaping your behavior toward positive goals. Don't allow yourself to indulge in them.

5. Look for the causes of your behavior in physical, social, economic, and political aspects of your current situation and not in personality defects in you.

6. Remind yourself that there are alternative views to every event. Reality is never more than shared agreements among people to call it the same way rather than as each one separately sees it. This enables you to be more tolerant in your interpretation of others' intentions and more generous in dismissing what might appear to be rejections or put-downs of you.

7. Never say bad things about yourself; especially, never attribute to yourself irreversible negative traits, like "stupid," "ugly," "uncreative," "a failure," "incorrigible."

---

[1] Reprinted from *Shyness: What It Is, What To Do About It* by Philip G. Zimbardo, copyright 1977, by permission of Addison-Wesley Publishing Co., Reading, Mass.

8. Don't allow others to criticize you as a person; it is your specific actions that are open for evaluation and available for improvement; accept such constructive feedback graciously if it will help you.

9. Remember that sometimes failure and disappointment are blessings in disguise, telling you the goals were not right for you, the effort was not worth it, and a bigger letdown later on may be avoided.

10. Do not tolerate people, jobs, and situations that make you feel inadequate. If you can't change them or yourself enough to make you feel more worthwhile, walk on out, or pass them by. Life is too short to waste time on downers.

11. Give yourself time to relax, to meditate, to listen to yourself, to enjoy hobbies and activities you can do alone. In this way, you can get in touch with yourself.

12. Practice being a social animal. Enjoy feeling the energy that other people transmit, the unique qualities and range of variability of our brothers and sisters. Imagine what their fears and insecurities might be and how you could help them. Decide what you need from them and what you have to give. Then, let them know that you are ready and open to sharing.

13. Stop being so overprotective about your ego; it is tougher and more resilient than you imagine. It bruises but never breaks. Better it should get hurt occasionally from an emotional commitment that didn't work out as planned, than get numbed from the emotional insulation of playing it too cool.

14. Develop long-range goals in life, with highly specific short-range subgoals. Develop realistic means to achieve these subgoals. Evaluate your progress regularly and be the first to pat yourself on the back or whisper a word of praise in your ear. You don't have to worry about being unduly modest if no one else hears you boasting.

15. You are not an object to which bad things just happen, a passive nonentity hoping, like a garden slug, to avoid being stepped on. You are the culmination of millions of years of evolution of our species, of your parents' dreams, of God's image. You are a unique individual who, as an active actor in life's drama, can make things happen. You can

change the direction of your entire life any time you choose to do so. With confidence in yourself, obstacles turn into challenges and challenges into accomplishments. Low self-esteem then recedes, because, instead of always preparing for and worrying about how you will live your life, you forget yourself as you become absorbed in the living of it.

ASSERTIVENESS TRAINING

AGENDA

   I. INTRODUCTION: GETTING ACQUAINTED AND SETTING
      OBJECTIVES

   II. GROUP DEFINITIONS OF ASSERTIVENESS

   III. MINI-LECTURE: NONASSERTION, AGGRESSION, AND
       ASSERTION—STYLES OF COMMUNICATION

   IV. MINI-LECTURE: VERBAL AND NONVERBAL CHARACTERIS-
       TICS OF NONASSERTION, AGGRESSION, AND ASSERTION

   V. EXERCISE: COMMUNICATION STYLES

   VI. MINI-LECTURE: SOME ASSERTIVE RIGHTS

       (Lunch)

   VII. ROLE PLAY: PRACTICING ASSERTIVE BEHAVIOR

  VIII. ROLE PLAY: BROKEN RECORD TECHNIQUE

   IX. ROLE PLAY: FOGGING TECHNIQUE

   X. SUMMING UP

   XI. EVALUATION OF WORKSHOP

I. INTRODUCTION: GETTING ACQUAINTED AND SETTING OBJECTIVES

Fill Out Name Tags
Ask participants to fill out name tags as they arrive and to list brief answers to the following questions:

• What is your definition of assertion?

• What things get in the way of personal growth—for example, what are
  some barriers to assertion?
•
• What do you hope to learn or accomplish today?

Introduce Yourself
Include your name, position, title; perhaps mention any formal or special training and background you have that are relevant to assertiveness training. Describe how you will be handling the role of leader; that you will be structuring the activities and acting as facilitator and resource person.

Purpose of Workshop
Share the following information, in your own words:

"This workshop is designed to help you understand and practice assertive social behavior. Assertiveness training is a process whereby one learns to replace self-defeating behavior with more satisfying, productive behavior. It is based on the theory that as one learns nonassertive or aggressive ways, one can also unlearn these negative habits and develop self-enhancing skills instead."

Overview of Workshop
"Today we will present some basic theory and techniques of assertiveness. There are many areas we cannot cover in so short a time, but with this introduction you can recognize and practice assertiveness. We will begin by defining what assertion is and how it differs from aggression and non-assertion. Next, we will teach you to distinguish among communication styles by noticing verbal and nonverbal behavioral cues. We will then discuss some barriers to assertion, some basic human rights, and how people keep from acting assertively. After each of you determines your particular problem areas in assertiveness, we will introduce some assertive techniques and have you practice them."

41

Setting Objectives

"At this point we'd like to give you a chance to meet one another and to find out what others hope to gain from today's experience. To accomplish this with a large crowd we use an exercise called Party Mix. Each of you filled out a name tag and answered three questions:

- "What is your definition of assertiveness?"

- "What things get in the way of growing?"

- "What do you hope to learn today?"

"I'd like you to put on your name tags and stand up. Mill around silently and read as many name tags as you can while others are reading yours. When we say stop, form groups with two people you don't know, then sit down with your group. (Allow 5 minutes for this part of exercise.)

"Now that you are in triads, please count off 1, 2, 3. Person 1 will begin by talking for one minute about some aspect of his or her name tag. When we call time, switch to person 2. Person 2 then has one minute to talk, then to person 3."

II. GROUP DEFINITIONS OF ASSERTIVENESS

Before explaining how assertion, aggression, and nonassertion differ, ask volunteers to share their definitions of assertiveness. List characteristics of assertion on a flipchart or chalkboard. Try to relate the group's definitions to the following mini-lecture.

III. MINI-LECTURE: NONASSERTION, AGGRESSION, AND ASSERTION—STYLES OF COMMUNICATION

"Borrowing from the work of Virginia Satir,[1] assertion can be defined as 'ideal or balanced communication.' If good communication is a two-way process involving the self, the content or message, and another person, communication that leaves out the self or the other is clearly unbalanced, much like a seesaw with only one rider. To understand this more clearly, let's look at two forms of unbalanced communication: nonassertion and aggression."

---

[1] Virginia Satir, *Peoplemaking*, Palo Alto, Calif.: Science and Behavior Books, 1972.

42

Nonassertion: Martyr

"A nonassertive communication leaves out the self. This happens when needs or feelings are not expressed and when you allow others to violate your rights. By concentrating totally on the other person's needs, wants, and desires, you leave out or subordinate your own needs. Not telling others what you need or feel, and hoping they will guess, leads others to make choices for you and allows you to be victimized (usually by an aggressive person). The unfortunate result of leaving out yourself is that your needs aren't met; how can others magically guess what you want all the time? Eventually you feel frustrated, disappointed, and resentful. Because others are running your life, you don't feel in control, and tend to suffer low self-esteem.

"People tend to act nonassertively to avoid unpleasantness or conflict. If you always give in and never express your needs, you may think that you are placating or keeping the peace. Unfortunately, attempts to avoid confrontation or tension are often made at the expense of a very important human being—you—and may invite others to walk over you and disdain you instead of like and respect you. Denying your own rights and needs is emotionally dishonest; manipulating others doesn't work either. Open and honest communication can only take place between self-respecting and respectful human beings.

"As an example of nonassertive behavior, imagine that a friend asks you what you'd like to do tonight. Although you would love to go out to dinner you answer, 'Whatever you'd like.' If the friend then asks, 'Would you rather see a movie or go dancing?,' you reply, 'You choose.'"

Aggression: Persecutor

"Aggression is often confused with assertion. However, an aggressive communication leaves out others' rights, feelings, and needs. Aggression is an act against others, whereby one person gets what he or she wants by dominating, manipulating, and humiliating others. Concentrating totally on your own needs and on what you want, you become insensitive to others in a hostile, offensive manner. In the short run, this type of behavior may bring results (getting the last piece of cake by grabbing it, for example), but it alienates people. In the long run you pay for disregarding others' rights, needs, and feelings. People don't enjoy being around someone who is self-righteous or angry, who puts them down or ignores their feelings.

"Many nonassertive people bottle up their feelings until they reach a breaking point. When they finally explode angrily in an aggressive outburst, they feel guilty and swing back to nonassertion. This seesawing from destructive passivity to attack is neither healthy nor satisfying.

"For example, after a frustrating day in which you have repressed your anger, someone bumps into you accidentally and you burst out, 'You stupid idiot, can't you watch where you're going?'"

Assertion: Balancer

"Assertive communication involves speaking up for yourself while considering the needs, wants, and rights of others. It is open and honest two-way communication, which enhances instead of hurts the communicators. It involves respecting your own and others' rights equally, and being responsible for your own behavior, running your own life, making your own choices. Assertive people are aware of others' rights and needs, do not always expect to get their way, and are willing to compromise. In the long run they do reach their goals, however, and they feel good about themselves because they have been open and honest with others.

"For example, instead of expressing anger when your child stays out late without calling, you say, 'When you are out late and don't call, I get very worried, so I would like you to call to say where you are if you're going to be out past 9:00 p.m.'"

IV. MINI-LECTURE: VERBAL AND NONVERBAL CHARACTERISTICS OF NONASSERTION, AGGRESSION, AND ASSERTION

"Awareness is the first step toward change, so I would like to help you learn about the verbal and nonverbal aspects of communication and how they affect assertiveness. Assertive messages are often 'muddied' by nonverbal cues. If you tremble, look at the ground, or stutter when you speak, the body sends out messages like, 'I'm scared, I'm shy, don't pay attention to me, I'm not important.' These nonverbal cues make the assertive message seem nonassertive. On the other hand, a loud voice, or a tense face or body, can make an assertive statement seem threatening, dominating, and aggressive.

"Nonverbal cues are so important to clear understanding that in books writers go out of their way to spell out how something was said. For example, 'Take it,' he said, slamming the book on the table angrily.

44

"Verbal characteristics of nonassertion include rambling, beating around the bush, apologizing profusely, not saying what you really feel or mean, saying nothing, letting things slide by without comment, being unclear. Nonverbal facial gestures, voice tone, eyes, and body position support a passive, frightened, or half-hearted verbal pattern. The body is slouched and needs support; eyes are downcast, tearful, or pathetic; hands are sticky or cold, clenching and unclenching nervously; the voice is soft, weak, unsteady; and the overall demeanor is one of hopeful pleading, a 'take-care-of-me-and-understand-my-needs-magically' look.

"Here is another example of nonassertion: a neighbor asks if you could possibly make a few wreaths for the Christmas Fair, since you made such a beauty for your own door last year. You pause for a long time (hoping she'll guess by your silence that you don't want to do it) and then say haltingly, 'Well, it is pretty difficult to find the materials, they're pretty rare.' Your friend brightly says, 'Oh, I'm sure you could find enough for a few wreaths.' 'Well, ah, I suppose I could get the materials,' you say, 'but when I'll have the time I don't know.' And you go on and on presenting one obstacle after another instead of saying directly that you don't want to do it.

"Appropriately assertive people state clearly, directly, and honestly what they are feeling. They use 'I' messages and say what they mean. Their general demeanor suggests assurance, understanding, and caring. Assertive people listen attentively and are warm and relaxed around others. They speak in a well-modulated, relaxed voice, and maintain good eye contact. An assertive stance is erect, balanced, and open to others. Here's an example of an assertive message: 'I really get angry when you stomp around and slam doors. If you're upset, I wish you'd talk to me about what's bothering you.'

"Aggressive actions include blaming, labeling, or accusing others. An air of superiority or one-upmanship often accompanies grand shows of strength or sarcasm. The voice is often loud, piercingly shrill, or chillingly cold and detached. Aggressive people look through you or stare blankly. The stone or grim face is accompanied by a rigid or haughty posture, which often leans into or over the other's space intrusively. The body's rigidity is expressed by jerky, dominating motions like table-pounding and finger-pointing. Example: 'You're absolutely hopeless! Here, I'll fix it.' "

V. EXERCISE: COMMUNICATION STYLES

Divide the group into pairs with persons "A" and "B." List the following sentences on a flipchart or chalkboard.

- I'm returning your sweater.
- Sure, you can borrow my car.
- I don't care.
- I really don't want to go.
- Isn't he handsome.
- I'd rather play tennis.

Have person A practice the first three sentences, saying each statement three ways (assertively, nonassertively, and aggressively) in any order. He or she should be aware of nonverbal cues and the messages they convey. Use exaggeration if necessary.

While A talks, B should listen carefully to voice tone and intensity, and notice the nonverbal body cues. He or she should then write down what communication style was used in each case, and what cues were given. After listening to each sentence spoken three ways, B should give A feedback on the nonverbal cues used.

Partners should then switch roles. Person B practices the last three sentences three ways, while person A tries to guess which style is being used.

VI. MINI-LECTURE: SOME ASSERTIVE RIGHTS

"In our society we believe that all people are created equal and therefore have certain inborn, inalienable rights. Rights are merely statements of basic human values that we espouse. They are something we give to ourselves and others, basic guidelines for acceptable human interaction. To act assertively, to stand up for your rights and honor other people's rights as well, you need to know what those rights are.

"*You have the right and responsibility to control your own life.*[1] Your basic constitutional rights to life, liberty, and the pursuit of happiness carry with them the responsibility to know and own yourself. Each person is a unique individual with the power to choose and make decisions based on his or her inner needs. No other person has the right to set your priorities or force you to do anything. You owe no explanations for your behavior, so long as you take responsibility for the consequences of your actions. Theoretically, you can do anything you want to do, as long as it doesn't hurt someone else. You have the right to behave in any manner you desire, realizing that others' rights to safety and security may lead them to curtail or punish dangerous behavior.

"*You have the right to hold and express your own feelings, thoughts, and opinions, and to be your own judge.* Every individual has the right to self-expression and fulfillment. Often people try to get someone to deny his or her feelings because that person's independence threatens them. Use of logic, 'shoulds,' and 'oughts' is often an attempt to control personal expression and to label something arbitrarily right or wrong. For example, the expression 'children should be seen and not heard' needs to be evaluated in light of your beliefs before you accept or reject it as a determinant of action.

"*You have the right to be treated respectfully and to be taken seriously.* Each person's uniqueness should be honored by others. You cannot expect others, however, to treat you with respect and take you seriously if you lack self-love and acceptance. You have to feel you deserve respect to get it.

"*You have the right to err and to change your mind.* Everyone makes mistakes. What's important is to learn from your mistakes and to use the experience for growth. The same goes for changing your mind. If you take responsibility for your decisions, then altering a decision when new facts or feelings arise is no crime or admission of wrongdoing, but rather, sensible behavior.

"*You have the right to be human (not perfect) and not to be liked by everyone.* People are finite and limited, so no one knows, understands, or even cares about everything. You don't need to be embarrassed about not being perfect in all areas; and it is possible to function well even with people who don't like you. Trying to please everyone leads to frustration and pleases no one, including yourself.

---

[1] This list of assertive rights is adapted from *The New Assertive Woman* by Lynn Z. Bloom, Karen Coburn, and Joan Pearlman. New York: Dell Publishing Co., 1976.

"You have the right to make and refuse requests without feeling guilty.
If you grant others the right to ask for favors, you need to grant that right
to yourself. Knowing that others have a right to refuse your legitimate requests means that you have the right to refuse also. Many people don't
ask for what they want out of fear of rejection or humiliation. They are
afraid to admit that, like other people, they have needs too. In fact, each
person's needs are very important and should be respected.

The right to ask includes asking others for information that you need
about yourself. Often people are intimidated by people who hold important roles or positions, and fear imposing on them or appearing ignorant.
Professionals (doctors, lawyers, accountants, social workers, etc.) are in
the business of providing services; you have the right to ask for any information about their services (costs, purpose, length of time, etc.), and to
be told what services they cannot provide. You have the right to shop
around and compare services, and to choose who your service provider
will be.

"You have the right to get what you pay for. This basic 'consumer' right
has been carefully protected by law as far as goods are concerned. When
purchasing services from professionals, as we said, you can shop and compare. You should always be clear what service you are contracting for.

"You have the right not to pursue a personal right. You need not feel
compelled to assert your rights at all times. As self-directing people, you
have the right to choose what you want to do. If you are too tired to
bother, don't care, or feel that the consequences of speaking up would
be too costly, you can choose not to assert yourself. This differs from
being nonassertive out of fear, because it is a conscious choice.

(Note to Leader: This may be a good point to break for lunch.)

VII. ROLE PLAY: PRACTICING ASSERTIVE BEHAVIOR

"Practicing assertion is one of the best ways to become truly assertive.
Taking on the role of an assertive person allows you to feel what happens
and to see that you can do it. Just as you learned to be nonassertive, you
can learn to be assertive by adding new, productive behaviors to your reper-

toire. Once experienced positively, new ways of acting become part of you. When you act differently, you are perceived differently and become different.

"Behavior rehearsal or 'role playing' is a basic technique to help you sharpen your skills. It forces you to clarify your assertive goals and helps you see where and how you sabotage yourself. Practicing sticky situations reduces anxiety and prepares you to tackle similar, real situations with confidence."

Role Play

Hand out the inventory entitled "Pinpointing Areas of Difficulty in Assertion" (see Handouts) and give participants 10 to 15 minutes to complete this part of the exercise. Also pass out the "Behavior Rehearsal Technique" sheet in the Handout section.

Arrange the group in triads and have them choose roles A, B, or C. (Each person will have a chance to play all three roles.) Person A will start off as the coach, B as the person trying to be appropriately assertive, and C as the responder or other party in the role play.

The Coach can stop the action anytime to consult with the responder on technique or to offer any suggestions that will help the asserter speak or act more assertively. The coach can suggest alternatives or compromises. Let the asserter know when he or she is being self-deprecating or getting sidetracked.

The Asserter should explain the details of the situation he or she wrote on the inventory to the other two people and then role play the same situation, with the person taking the role of the responder, or other party. This time the asserter should try to act as a truly assertive person, using nonverbal body cues as well as words.

There are several things the asserter should keep in mind:

- What is the goal of this assertion? What am I trying to accomplish?

- What are the barriers to acting assertively? (anxiety, habit, fears, shoulds, or oughts)

- What are my rights in this situation?

• Some things to concentrate on during the role play are:

    —sitting or standing in an alert, attentive position that commands respect;
    —breathing well and speaking in a relaxed, easy manner;
    —looking at the person I'm addressing;
    —acknowledging that I hear and understand what the other person says;
    —expressing my thoughts and feelings clearly.

The Responder plays the role of the other person in the situation, keeping as close to the original situation as possible.

Allow two to five minutes for the role play; then persons B and C should switch roles and replay the scene. Next, switch so that B plays asserter again, with the coach as responder and the responder as coach.

Set 1	**Set 2**	**Set 3**
A — Coach	A — Coach	A — Responder
B — Asserter	B — Responder	B — Asserter
C — Responder	C — Asserter	C — Coach

After three rounds of role playing the same situation, ask the group to evaluate the assertions, using the following questions as guidelines:

• Did I (the asserter) achieve my goal, say what I wanted to say, get my point across?

• Was I direct and honest?

• Did I stand up for my rights without violating the rights of others?

• Was my posture assertive?

• Was my voice strong, calm, and relaxed?

• In what ways could I improve my assertiveness?

Help the group process what happens. You may want to role play an assertion that baffled the group, as it is important to role play to a positive conclusion. Having the original asserter then play him- or herself with you afterward is often helpful.

Repeat the process with person A as the asserter, B the responder, and C the coach. Person A should draw the situation from his or her inventory.

Set 1	Set 2	Set 3
A – Asserter	A – Responder	A – Asserter
B – Responder	B – Asserter	B – Coach
C – Coach	C – Coach	C – Responder

Then conduct a round with person C as the asserter, using a situation from his or her inventory.

Set 1	Set 2	Set 3
A – Coach	A – Coach	A – Responder
B – Responder	B – Asserter	B – Coach
C – Asserter	C – Responder	C – Asserter

VIII. ROLE PLAY: BROKEN RECORD TECHNIQUE

"This is a technique to enable you to hold your ground with manipulative people. It teaches you to stick to your point without being swayed by manipulative logic, evasion of responsibility, or statements meant to make you feel guilty or stupid. It helps you to reach your goal or a reasonable compromise, and to get the manipulator to stop controlling the situation.

"In conflict situations, you need to remain calm and relaxed enough to stick to your point. Manipulative people will try their best to get you to give up by using a variety of ploys: 'You're holding up the line'; 'we only sell these'; 'the factory warrants the product'; 'we can't help you'; 'what do you mean it's too big, it looks fine to me.' These ploys are meant to make you feel responsible for the problems or wrong in your judgment. Usually the manipulator tries the old 'pass-the-buck' routine to avoid responsibility, or explains why you can't do what you want. Since we are all brought up to listen and be polite, we tend to get caught up in the words and can be swayed from our purpose. If you remember your assertive rights, you don't need to offer excuses for your behavior or justify why you are doing something. To let people know that nothing they say will make you go away without getting what you came for, the broken record is very effective.

"Decide what your goal is. If, for example, you are returning a defective toaster, do you want a new toaster, or do you want it fixed free, or do you want your money back? (Be sure to read any warranties before deciding what you're entitled to do.) Put your request into one or two sentences and keep repeating those sentences over and over, ignoring all ploys and side issues brought up by the manipulator. Concentrate on your sentences and keep saying them in a calm, repetitive voice until you get what you want or get an acceptable compromise. Usually, after three or four ploys have failed, the other person realizes he or she must deal with you and gives up."

Example

"You bought a toaster two days ago and after you used it a few times it stopped working. The toaster came with a one-year guarantee. You go to the store where you purchased it, having decided that you want a replacement. Your broken record sentences might be, 'I bought this toaster here two days ago and it is defective. It has a one-year guarantee, I would like a replacement toaster.' The salesclerk looks at it and says, 'Well, it's been used, we can't take that back.' (Attempting to make you feel guilty.) Ignoring this comment you repeat: 'I bought this toaster here two days ago. It's defective, has a one-year guarantee, and I'd like a replacement.' The clerk says, 'Look, we can't send a used toaster back to the manufacturer.' (Attempting to make you responsible for the store's problem.) So you add, 'I'm really not interested in the store's problems with defective merchandise. I would like a replacement for this toaster, which is defective and guaranteed for one year.' 'Well,' says the clerk, 'I really can't take any more time with you, I have six customers waiting in line.' (Another attempt to make you responsible for the store's problems.) You reply, 'If you would satisfy my request quickly, the others won't have to wait so long. I bought this toaster two days ago. It's defective and I want a replacement.' The clerk, finally realizing that you won't be put off, says, 'Well, okay. Give me your sales slip and I'll write up an exchange.' 'Thank you,' you say politely."

Role Play

Have the group divide into pairs and choose roles A or B. For the first role play, A is the asserter and B the manipulator; then partners switch roles for the second role play. Have the pairs act out the following situations.

1. Door-to-door encyclopedia salesman.
   The asserter is not interested in buying encyclopedias, and says, "I understand, but I'm not interested in buying."
   The manipulator is a very persistent salesman who tries every angle: asking about the kids, whether he can use your bathroom, etc.

2. Returning a defective battery, after three months, that is guaranteed for six years.

52

The asserter says, "I have a six-year guarantee. I've had this battery for three months and it's broken. I want a new battery."
The manipulator, the complaint department man, tries to put off the asserter with every trick he knows.

IX. ROLE PLAY: FOGGING TECHNIQUE

"This is a good technique to use when you are being criticized or made to feel guilty or anxious. Criticism is meant to make you feel bad, and it usually causes a defensive retort leading to a fight. Fogging helps break the manipulative cycle and forces the criticizer to stop picking on you.

"Most of us become upset and defensive when criticized. Our emotional distress pleases the persecutor. If we don't react to the underlying implications of wrongdoing and remain calm, the persecutor has nothing to work with and ceases.

"Fogging is accomplished by responding verbally to criticism as if you are a dense fog bank: you let the criticism go through you without offering resistance. You do this by listening carefully to the critical words and agreeing with any hint of truth in them. Unfortunately, all criticism has some truth to it, which is why people tend to become defensive and to counterattack. People suddenly feel guilty when they see that something is or could be true. It is natural to think you have done something wrong in these circumstances and to try to defend your actions or criticize the persecutor to even things up. This leads to conflict, which usually makes matters worse. Acting like a fog bank enables you to react to what the persecutor says while letting the innuendo of wrongdoing go right through you like a rock hauled through the fog. It means not being hurt by criticism, and accepting the fact that, like everyone else, you may have some faults or make mistakes, but so what."

Example
"Helen is always on a diet. One day she's having lunch with a friend who says, 'Helen, that's the second piece of bread you've had.' Responding only to the critical words, not to the emotional reaction they trigger, Helen says, 'Yes, it is the second piece of bread I've had.' The friend logically and righteously says, "Well, isn't that a very fattening food?" Helen fogs again, 'You're right, bread is very fattening.' She responds to the words, but offers no defense or excuse for her behavior."

Role Play

Have the group divide again into pairs. Person A will be the Critical Persecutor, and person B will be the Fogger.

Person A criticizes some aspect of B's appearance, habits, or personality, and persists until he or she is blocked by fogging.

Person B assertively "fogs" the critical comments by listening carefully to the words used (ignoring the negative implications) and agreeing with any real or possible truth in the statements.

After one role play A and B switch roles.

X. SUMMING UP

"Today we have given you a basic introduction to assertiveness training. First we talked about three communication styles and defined assertion as balanced, open, and honest communication. We reviewed nonverbal aspects of assertion, nonassertion, and aggression, and talked about how body language can clarify or muddy assertion. Then we practiced using nonverbal cues three ways and discussed some basic assertive rights.

"This afternoon, each of you pinpointed particular areas that cause you great difficulty and then practiced using the behavior rehearsal technique. We wrapped up the day by presenting two other techniques to use with people who are being aggressive or critical. There is obviously much more material that we couldn't cover in one day. We hope that you will take a longer assertiveness training course, or read some of the books on our handout and keep practicing and growing."

XI. EVALUATION OF WORKSHOP

Hand out 3 x 5" cards or paper for the evaluation.

"We have enjoyed working with you today, and hope you will join us for other workshops. We would like your reactions to the experience, and would appreciate it if you would answer the following questions:

54

• "What is your assessment of the workshop? How could it be improved?

• "How would you describe the style and effectiveness of the leaders?

• "What did you learn about yourself and others today?"

Ask participants to turn in their evaluations. You may want to announce any upcoming groups or workshops that people may be interested in, and pass out the handouts at this time.

HANDOUTS FOR

ASSERTIVENESS TRAINING

NONASSERTION, AGGRESSION, AND ASSERTION[1]

Nonassertion: Martyr

Leaves self out by not expressing needs or feelings or by denying or letting others violate his or her rights.

Why?:   To avoid unpleasantness or conflict.

Results: Needs aren't met; frustration, disappointment, and low self-esteem.

Aggression: Persecutor

Leaves out others' rights, feelings, and needs. Acts against others by getting what he or she wants by dominating, manipulating, and humiliating others.

Why?:   To reach immediate goals, to express anger.

Results: Accomplishes short-term goals but alienates others, ends up lonely and bitter.

Assertion: Balanced Communicator

Speaks up for self appropriately while considering the needs, wishes, and rights of others. Practices open, honest, two-way communication.

Why?:   To communicate effectively, feel good about self.

Results: May not reach short-range goals, may compromise or go for alternatives, usually reaches long-term goals, has healthy relationships, and feels good about self for being open and honest with others.

---

[1] Adapted from *Peoplemaking* by Virginia Satir. Palo Alto, Calif.: Science and Behavior Books, 1972.

VERBAL AND NONVERBAL CHARACTERISTICS OF THREE COMMUNICATION STYLES

NONASSERTION

Verbal: rambling, beating around the bush, overapologizing, not saying what he or she really feels.

Nonverbal: slouched posture; downcast, averted, or tearful eyes; sticky or cold hands; nervous gestures; soft, weak, pleading, or unsteady voice; overall demeanor says, "take care of me."

AGGRESSION

Verbal: blaming or accusing others; displays sarcasm, an air of superiority.

Nonverbal: makes shows of strength; has a loud or brittle voice; a cold, detached look; rigid or haughty posture; jerky, dominating gestures like finger-pointing, table-pounding; intrudes into others' space.

ASSERTION

Verbal: clear, direct, honest statement of feelings; use of "I" messages.

Nonverbal: listens well to others; upright posture; speaks in a relaxed, well-modulated voice; maintains good eye contact.

SOME ASSERTIVE RIGHTS

1. You have the right and responsibility to control your own life.

2. You have the right to hold and express your own feelings, thoughts, and opinions and to be your own judge.

3. You have the right to be treated with respect and to be taken seriously.

4. You have the right to err and to change your mind.

5. You have the right to be human (not perfect) and not to be liked by everyone.

6. You have the right to make and refuse requests without feeling guilty.

7. You have the right to get what you pay for.

8. You have the right to choose not to pursue a personal right.

PINPOINTING AREAS OF DIFFICULTY IN ASSERTION

Below are listed different situations that many people find difficult to handle assertively. Please go down the list and check those areas that cause you considerable difficulty. Next, circle three that are most difficult, then choose one area that you'd like to work on in a role play. Write five sentences on the back of the sheet describing a recent situation where you were nonassertive in that area.

**Areas of Considerable
Difficulty**

Dealing with aggressive people.

Saying no to a persuasive salesman.

Asking someone who is disturbing me to stop.

Returning faulty merchandise to the store.

Making requests or asking favors or help.

Refusing reasonable requests.

Praising others or accepting compliments.

Expressing affection, tenderness, or love.

Expressing anger.

Beginning or maintaining conversations.

Reprimanding unfair treatment.

Criticizing inferior work.

Making decisions.

Speaking up in close relationships.

Containing feelings and then exploding.

Expressing feelings.

Conversing in groups.

Maintaining a satisfactory social life.

Being assertive on the job.

BEHAVIOR REHEARSAL TECHNIQUE

Preparation for Role Play

1. What is the goal of this assertion? What am I trying to accomplish?

2. What are the barriers to acting assertively? (anxiety, habit, fears, shoulds, or oughts)

3. What are my rights in this situation?

4. Some things to concentrate on during role play are—

   • sitting or standing in an alert, attentive position that commands respect;

   • breathing well and speaking in a relaxed manner;

   • looking at the person I'm addressing;

   • acknowledging that I hear and understand what the other person says;

   • expressing my feelings clearly.

Evaluation of Assertion

1. Did I achieve my goal, say what I wanted to say, get my point across assertively?

2. Was I direct and honest?

3. Did I stand up for my rights without violating the rights of others?

4. Was my posture assertive?

5. Was my voice strong, calm, and relaxed?

6. Ways I could improve my assertiveness are . . .

CREATIVE CONTACT FOR SINGLES

AGENDA

   I. INTRODUCTION: GETTING ACQUAINTED AND SETTING OBJECTIVES

  II. EXERCISE: THE ADVANTAGES OF BEING SINGLE

 III. MINI-LECTURE: HOW THE ETERNAL SEARCH FOR THE "ONE AND ONLY" PREVENTS YOU FROM GETTING THE MOST OUT OF YOUR SINGLE EXPERIENCE

 IV. MINI-LECTURE AND EXERCISES: SOME CONVERSATION DEVELOPMENT TECHNIQUES

     (Lunch)

  V. MINI-LECTURE: THE ART OF DEVELOPING FRIENDSHIPS

 VI. EXERCISE: TAKING STOCK

VII. MINI-LECTURE: RESOURCES FOR SINGLES

VIII. EXERCISE: SHARING RESOURCES

 IX. EXERCISE: DEVELOPING AN AREA OF INTEREST

  X. EVALUATION OF WORKSHOP AND SUMMING UP

I. INTRODUCTION: GETTING ACQUAINTED AND SETTING OBJECTIVES

Fill Out Name Tags

Ask participants to fill out name tags as they arrive and to list brief answers to the following questions. Post questions where everyone can see them.

• What do you like about being single?

• What barriers do you feel keep you from enjoying being single?

• What do you hope to learn or accomplish today?

Introduce Yourself

Include your name, position, and title, and perhaps mention any formal education and special training relevant to leading this workshop. Use of personal information is up to you.

Describe how you will be handling the role of the leader: structuring sessions, acting as a facilitator and resource person and, if there are two leaders, what each of you will be doing.

Purpose of Workshop

Share the following information in your own words: "Many more people are single today and many feel isolated in our traditionally coupled society. Due to myths and prejudices, many singles fail to develop their own potential while searching for a quick escape from being single instead of enjoying it. We hope today to begin showing you how satisfying and delightful being single can be."

Overview of Workshop

Display the agenda on a flipchart or chalkboard and briefly review the topics to be covered.

Setting Objectives

"At this point I'd like you to meet one another and find out what people hope to gain from today's experience. To accomplish this with a large crowd, I use an exercise called Party Mix. Each of you filled out a name tag and answered three questions:

- What do you like about being single?
- What keeps you from enjoying being single?
- What do you hope to learn today?

Now I'd like you to stand up. Mill around silently and read others' name tags while they read yours. When I call stop, choose two people you don't know, form a group, and sit down. (Allow 5 minutes, then call 'stop.')

"Now that you're in triads, please count off 1, 2, 3. Person 1 will now spend one minute talking about what he or she thinks are the advantages of being single and his or her reasons for coming today. Then person 2 has one minute, then person 3."

II. EXERCISE: THE ADVANTAGES OF BEING SINGLE

Group Responses
"Most of you are probably very conscious of the disadvantages of being single, but I wonder how many of you ever stop to think about the positives? We've asked you to list both positives and negatives, so you could see the pros and cons of singlehood. Now we'd like to make a master list of the advantages singles can enjoy."

As leader, solicit responses and record them on a chalkboard or flipchart. Some advantages people usually mention are: independence, being free to come and go as I want, being able to date who I please, having control of my own money, choices, freedom from having to fill certain roles and from others' expectations of me, privacy, lack of commitment, flexibility, solitude, ability to maintain a variety of friendships with both sexes, being able to be as neat or sloppy as I want. Add any to the list that the group omits.

Summary
"There are many positive reasons to choose to be single. Freedom, economic and emotional autonomy, and unlimited opportunities for meeting new people and experiencing life are often highlighted by happy singles. Not being tied to one role—breadwinner or wife, for example, and not having family responsibilities are also important factors to many people.

"Singlehood is now a positive alternative to marriage, as one can find emotional support, an active social life, and sex without the traditional constraints of marriage. It is a situation that stimulates growth and fulfill-ment—truly something one can choose and feel good about.

"Freedom is the benefit single people mention most often. One has choices that marriage or exclusive relationships hinder. The only restric-tions on where one goes and with whom are chosen by the single person, not imposed by others. The growing feeling that marriage restricts one's growth is the major reason many people make a conscious choice to re-main single. The old failure factors like parent fixation, unattractiveness, lack of proficiency in the dating game, unrealistic expectations, etc., are not the reasons many give for rejecting marriage today. In fact, many peo-ple who are single by choice are proficient socializers and have rejected the mating game as meaningless."

III. MINI-LECTURE: HOW THE ETERNAL SEARCH FOR THE "ONE AND ONLY" PREVENTS YOU FROM GETTING THE MOST OUT OF YOUR SINGLE EXPERIENCE

"A myth that we have been brought up with is that for each of us there exists a 'one and only' who is meant for us. The fairytale tells us that once we find the 'right' person, our troubles will be over and we'll live 'happily ever after.' It is true that a happy marriage provides much satisfac-tion, but eternally searching for a magic answer in another person causes us to neglect our own development and rarely works. Many singles become miserable when following a program meant to snare their 'one and only'; they feel a terrible emptiness in their lives. If the search has driven you to make major life decisions based on meeting someone rather than on your own interests, you have probably experienced gnawing dissatisfaction.

"Looking outside yourself for fulfillment is the major reason the eternal search fails. Instead of developing his or her own potentials and interests, the searcher remains an incomplete person looking for another half. Pur-suing one goal so hard leaves little time to enjoy life, and often the effort leads to tension and drives people away. Concentrating on finding a mate leads to a lopsided and dissatisfactory life-style.

"Whether you are single or married, you need to take responsibility for your own happiness before you will be happy with another person. If you feel incomplete and unhappy as a single, you're not likely to be attractive to others, who see you looking to them to 'fill you up.' You have little to offer others except your needs and desires. Only by relaxing the search and developing your own personality can you become a whole, happy, person capable of giving and taking freely in a healthy relationship with another."

IV. MINI-LECTURE AND EXERCISES: SOME CONVERSATION DEVELOPMENT TECHNIQUES

Introduction

"To move beyond the search for the 'one and only' and be a more balanced single person, one has to learn to reach out to others in many social settings. In the old days, people lived in one spot, and their social networks were ready-made. In our mobile society, one often faces new situations with no familiar people around, and must learn to make new friends and communicate comfortably, in order not to feel isolated.

"While these exercises build on the obvious skills that many of you already have, we are practicing them with you today to demonstrate how easy it is to meet and converse with other single adults, even in large groups where most people feel intimidated.

Conversation Skills

Initiating and Maintaining Conversations
"Contrary to popular opinion, you do not need a smooth preplanned opener to start a conversation. You do need the desire to communicate and someone willing to engage in conversation with you. The first step is to select someone who looks available (not wrapped up in work or deeply involved with someone else) and approachable. (Often this is someone who is alone or wandering about.)"

Self-Disclosure
"One of the easiest ways to start a conversation is by offering some information about yourself. This can be an expanded introduction: 'I'm Susan, I just moved in here.' Or a self-disclosing statement: 'I really love tennis.' Or, 'This is the first time I have been on a plane.'

72

Following the Other's Self-Disclosure
"Other people constantly give out information about their feelings, their interests, hopes, dreams, and worries, what they do, what they want out of life. This free information often indicates what is important to them and is ideal to follow up on. If I say, 'I'm new in this area.' I've given you some free information about myself. Using this as a clue to a present concern, you might say, 'How long has you lived here?' 'Where did you move from?' 'How do you like it here?' 'Have you met many of your neighbors yet?' This tells me you are listening and are interested in me, and encourages me to tell you more about myself. By practicing self-disclosure and following up on other people's free information, you can start and maintain a lively conversation. The one exception might be when the person you're attempting to converse with offers no information or response beyond a 'yes' or 'no' in return."

Exercise: Initiating and Maintaining a Conversation

"Please pick a partner you don't know well and sit down facing that person. Choose A and B. Person A initiates a conversation with B by sharing some information (self-disclosure) in one of the following settings (tell your partner which setting you chose before beginning): a bus, classroom, or meeting. Person B follows up on A's self-disclosure and tries to maintain the conversation without sharing information about him- or herself. Switch roles and have Person B pick one of the settings A didn't choose. (Allow 2-3 minutes for each conversation.)

"As you probably realize from doing this exercise, simply following up on someone's self-disclosure, without offering any information about yourself, can be very stilted and unrewarding. The person who is sharing begins to feel he or she is being pumped or interrogated.

"This time, have Person B start a conversation in one of the following settings: a movie line, at work, or in a store. As Person A follows up on the self-disclosure, add something about yourself. After B's turn, switch roles." (Allow 2-3 minutes for each conversation.)

(Note to Leader: Many people utilize these skills unconsciously. For others, understanding how easy it is to follow up on others' cues is a revelation, and being able to chatter with another person is a new and positive

73

experience. Suggest that members practice these skills outside the group until the skills become second nature. Initiating and maintaining conversations are skills many people lack, and these simple exercises can help them become more relaxed and open with people in social settings.)

Exercise: Joining and Leaving Conversations

"Many of us feel comfortable one-to-one but are overwhelmed when we don't know anyone. We usually feel worse if everyone else is already engaged in conversation when we arrive.

"There are a few steps you can take to join a conversation comfortably. The same principle of following up on freely disclosed information applies. In order to hear what is being said, you need to get close to the other people who are talking and listen. In the same way that you would start a conversation by following up on your partner's self-disclosure, make a statement that elaborates on a remark made and add some information about yourself. 'I had the same problems with my car until I found the greatest mechanic . . . ' " Once you are in the group, continue to follow up and add information to maintain the conversation.

"Often how you end a conversation makes or breaks the next contact with a person or group. When you wish to move on, you need to take the other person's feelings into account. Even if you don't wish to speak with the person again, courtesy is always best. You can ask that person to join you as you move to another conversation by saying, 'Sounds like they're discussing something interesting, shall we go join them?' or, 'Let's go join them. I'd like to hear what they have to say.' Other ways to move are to excuse yourself and state where you're going. 'Excuse me, I see an old friend over there who I'd like to catch' or 'I think I'll go get some cheese and crackers.' Sometimes you have to leave a conversation that you really enjoyed. You may want to add, 'I've really enjoyed talking with you.' If you would like to see the person again, you might add, 'I'd like to get to know you better, I do hope we'll meet again.' "

Have everyone stand up. Then arrange the group into triads. Have each group number itself 1, 2, 3 and instruct persons 1 and 2 to start a conversation. The third person should approach the dyad from another part of the room, and join the conversation. This involves placing oneself close enough to the conversation to hear what is being said—that is, being peripheral before entering the conversation. Being present but not included is often a painful experience for people who don't know how to break into a conversation, and the normalcy of this as a stage prior to entering needs to be pointed out. Once this is practiced, it becomes more natural and shouldn't evoke anxiety.

After person 3 has joined the conversation, person 1 should leave that triad and join another group in conversation. When that person joins, person 1 from that group should join the group the new person left. Repeat this process until everyone has joined an ongoing conversation and returned to his or her original group. Next, have person number 1 initiate a move of the whole triad to another triad. This finishes the practice progression and gives everyone a chance to join a conversation and then for a small group to join another group. (Allow 10 to 12 minutes for this exercise.)

This exercise gets group members up and moving around, and simulates the feeling of a party or social gathering. Members usually respond well to it and are often proud to discover they can join a conversation and bring others with them to a new and larger group.

(Note to Leader: You may want to break for lunch at this point.)

V. MINI-LECTURE: THE ART OF DEVELOPING FRIENDSHIPS

"There are many definitions of friendship. The important idea to keep in mind is that we all need friends with whom we can share experiences, thoughts, and ideas. If you aren't satisfied with the number or quality of friends you have now, you must decide that you want new friends. Having people we respond to and who respond to us, with whom we can share our joys and sorrows, can make the difference between enjoying being single and feeling miserable.

"It is helpful, then, to ponder what friendship means to us—in other words, what value we place on friends and what needs friendships can fill. Companionship and sharing are two aspects that are very important in a relationship.

"Doing things together and spending time together are the foundations of friendship. If you think about this, it makes sense. It is hard to start or keep a friendship going if no time together is planned. This means that if you want more or better friendships, you must take steps to find people who meet your needs and have time available to spend with you. Regular contact and involvement in enjoyable activities allow for other aspects of friendship to gain strength. Intensity is built this way, and acceptance, sharing of feelings, being comfortable, and a sense of belonging follow.

"Once you know what your needs are and what interests and preferences you have, it becomes a question of going where people are, doing things you enjoy, and becoming involved or inviting others to share some enjoyable experience with you. This means risking getting hurt or being turned down once in a while. If you decide not to reach out and stay home with your TV, you are playing a no-win game. There is no chance of starting or building a successful relationship. If you do get out and get involved, you have raised your chances at least 50 percent. Of course, you can fail, but chances are you won't; and 50 percent is better than zero. Friendships are hard work, but unless you're a hermit, it's worth it to be and have a friend with whom you can share joys, accomplishments, and confidences.

"Some things you can do to build up your friendships are: a) decide you want friends; b) be your own best friend by building up your confidence and accepting yourself as a good and worthwhile person (this involves realizing that you can enjoy yourself and focusing on your strengths and good qualities instead of your faults and lacks); c) learn some social skills if you are uncomfortable talking about yourself or holding a conversation; d) decide that you like people and try to make them comfortable and happy when you're around; e) take the initiative: get out, take risks, put yourself out for others, and be thoughtful (remember that focusing inward too much makes one depressed and that happy people tend to focus outward); f) be a friend; this means being sensitive to another person's needs and being there when needed, to share good times and bad.

"If you don't put time and effort into a relationship, or if you criticize and argue and don't communicate or share, you'll find the quality of friendship slipping.

"Most people require a variety of relationships to fill their needs and to keep their lives meaningful and growing. The tendency of many single people is to focus so hard on finding one other special person—a mate—that they neglect other relationships and end up feeling lonely and frustrated. Expecting any one person to fill all your social needs is unrealistic and bound to fail. Many couples fall into the trap of feeling they should relate only to each other; soon they find themselves bored and then resentful that their needs aren't being met. We all need other people with whom we can socialize, share hobbies or interests, talk deeply, simply go to a play or movie. No one person can or should be expected to meet all of your needs. Successful single people usually have a variety of people with whom they share ideas, interests, activities, and confidences. Most people have a few close friends and several acquaintances. As we said before, the basis for any friendship is built on time spent together, so a multitude of close relationships would be almost impossible to maintain. It isn't the quantity of relationships that counts but the quality. A few good friends who meet your needs and enrich life and foster your growth are far better than a multitude of 'should' relationships or people you don't enjoy very much.

"Many singles cheat themselves by restricting themselves to same-sex friends. There are many pressures set up by our society that make people believe men and women can't be friends without sex entering into the scene. This myth keeps us stuck playing games by treating each other as sex objects (pursuer or bait) instead of as human beings. Men and women can enjoy affectionate relationships without sexual involvement, and opening your mind to this possibility can enrich your life. Being able to choose friends from either sex broadens your source of friendships, allows you to learn how people of the opposite sex feel, and to be more natural and relaxed with the opposite sex. Having opposite-sex friends you can take to events also helps you stay cool and be less panicked about finding a mate.

"Developing platonic friendships takes the same time and effort as other relationships. If you've never had an opposite-sex friend, you may want to think why you don't try having one. Obviously, there are times when one party or the other wants a sexual relationship, but there are also times when platonic relationships are appropriate and even preferable. The key to establishing and maintaining platonic relationships is open and honest communication between the parties in negotiating what type of relationship they would like."

VI. EXERCISE: TAKING STOCK

Introduction
"Occasionally, it is helpful to pause in our busy lives and evaluate where we are and whether the path we've been treading is satisfying or not. We may find that we're maintaining relationships that we feel we 'should' keep, or relating to a role rather than a person, or finding that once meaningful relationships have soured as we've grown and changed. We may be

stagnating and feeling blue because we're hanging on to friendships that no longer fill our needs. People do change, and relationships that were once satisfying may be maintained out of nostalgia, laziness, or feelings of loyalty. These relationships use up a lot of energy, and keep us from establishing more relevant and growth-producing relationships.

"The exercise that we're going to do now will give you the opportunity to evaluate your pattern of relationships. Once again, self-awareness precedes action; we must know how we feel. Each of us has the power within us to change our patterns toward growth and fulfillment."

Exercise
"List 5-10 people you consider friends, then list five acquaintances. From your friendship list, pick the person who makes you feel best when you are around him or her. Now pick the person who makes you feel the worst. Take all the other names on your two lists and put them under the first two names you picked. You now have two columns, one listing the people who uplift you and the other, people who deflate you or bring you down. Now pick one of the acquaintances from the uplift list. Acquaintances can become friends, and this is a good place to begin if you want to expand your social network."

As leader, divide the group into pairs and have them choose A or B. Instruct person A to speak for one minute on what steps he or she could take to develop an acquaintance into a friendship. Person B can then give A feedback and suggestions. Then switch roles and repeat the process.

VII. MINI-LECTURE: RESOURCES FOR SINGLES

Note to leader: Before the workshop begins, assemble and make into a visual display various resources from your area. These might include: a list of singles clubs; publications for singles; other social or educational groups; dating services; groups formed around particular interests or activities such as sports, the arts, politics, conservation; and places to go and things to do in your area, including musical events, museums, sports arenas, restaurants, colleges, and parks.

"Now that we've shed our bad attitudes about being single, let's talk about where we can meet people who might become friends. With 43 million other singles, it should be simple to meet people we like, but it isn't, especially in large cities. It is possible, but you have to stick your neck out. Meeting new people is a problem not only for people who have never been married but also for the divorced and widowed adults who now make up half of the singles population. Newly divorced or widowed people, totally out of circulation for ten or twenty years, often have no idea how to go about meeting other unmarrieds, whereas never-marrieds have often had a lot of practice in developing friendships and knowing where to meet people.

"At any rate, if you want to meet other people, you must realize that single people are everywhere, and that your attitude is the important determinant of how successful you're going to be. 'Unseek and you shall find' could well be a singles motto; oddly enough, not consciously seeking 'the one and only' is the best way to meet people and has worked time and time again.

"Focus on what you're doing and how much you enjoy it, not on who you can meet. Relax and you'll be more responsive to whatever the experience brings you. You may meet someone special, make a new friend, or meet no one.

"I'm going to talk with you about activities specifically geared to singles so that you can evaluate the pros and cons of each and see if you would like to try any of them. Then we'll have time to discuss other resources that you've found particularly enjoyable."

VIII. EXERCISE: SHARING RESOURCES

"Becoming involved in activities that reflect our interests is a great way to meet kindred spirits. If you enjoy hiking, for instance, you can easily find out where there are others who share this interest by looking at your local newspaper or the yellow pages of your phone book for the name, address, and phone number of a club near you.

"Volunteer organizations are another source for new contacts. Working with others on a task is a great way to get to know people, and almost every nonprofit group will welcome you with open arms. Recreational groups and adult education centers also offer a variety of activities you might enjoy.

"Deciding that you'll get out and take a few risks is your best bet in reaching out to others. You can meet new friends at the laundromat, at work, or even standing in line at the bank. Your own openness and willingness to get involved are your keys to success.

"I'd like each of you to write down a resource or an activity that you've enjoyed on the back of your name tag. (Allow 1-2 minutes for group to write.)

"Now, I'd like all of you to stand up, take a nice stretch, then pick 5 other people near you and form a group. Next, pick a recorder. This person's job is to list all the resources his or her group developed. (Allow 5 minutes.)

"Now I'd like the recorders to read the resources to me so that I can list them on the flipchart. (Ask for additional information if needed, and list resources on flipchart or chalkboard. Suggest that people note down resources they might want to investigate.)"

IX. EXERCISE: DEVELOPING AN AREA OF INTEREST

"Now that we've shared ideas about places and activities, I'd like each of you to close your eyes and think of one interest or activity that you could pursue. (Allow 1-2 minutes.)

"Divide your group of 6 into 3 pairs. Members of each pair should choose to be A or B. Person A will have one minute to tell person B how he or she might get involved in the interest or activity he or she picked."

X. EVALUATION OF WORKSHOP AND SUMMING UP

"To help us improve the workshop and our leadership style, and to help you evaluate what you've learned, we'd like you to take 5 minutes now to answer three questions."

Pass out cards or paper and list the following questions on the chalkboard or flipchart:

• What is your evaluation of the workshop? Any suggestions?

• How would you comment on the style and effectiveness of the leaders?

• What did you learn about yourself and others today?

80

"This brings our program for today to an end. We've enjoyed running the workshop and hope that you also benefited from participating."

(Optional) "As our goodbye gift, we have a list of some activities going on in our area this evening, that some of you may be interested in attending." (Prepare a list of happenings in your city or area and list them on a flipchart. Often, workshop participants ask for this kind of information and several people begin expanding their social network immediately as a result of the workshop.)

Pass out any handouts as participants leave. Besides the handout on communication development techniques, which follows, you might want to pass out the list of resources you prepared for the workshop.

HANDOUTS FOR

CREATIVE CONTACT FOR SINGLES

SOME CONVERSATION DEVELOPMENT TECHNIQUES

Initiating and Maintaining Conversations

Contrary to popular opinion, you do not need a smooth preplanned opener to start a conversation. You do need the desire to communicate and someone willing to engage in conversation with you. The first step is to select someone who looks available (not wrapped up in work or deeply involved with someone else) and approachable. (Often this is someone who is alone or wandering about.)

Self-Disclosure

One of the easiest ways to start a conversation is by offering some information about yourself. This can be an expanded introduction: "I'm Susan, I just moved in here." Or a self-disclosing statement: "I really love tennis." Or, "This is the first time I have been on a plane."

Following the Other's Self-Disclosure

Other people constantly give out information about their feelings, their interests, hopes, dreams, and worries, what they do, what they want out of life. This free information often indicates what is important to them and is ideal to follow up on. If I say, "I'm new in this area," I've given you some free information about myself. Using this as a clue to a present concern, you might say, "How long have you lived here?" "Where did you move from?" "How do you like it here?" "Have you met many of your neighbors yet?" This tells me you are listening and are interested in me, and encourages me to tell you more about myself. By practicing self-disclosure and following up on other people's free information, you can start and maintain a lively conversation. The one exception might be when the person you're attempting to converse with offers no information or response beyond a "yes" or "no" in return.

STRESS MANAGEMENT

AGENDA

  I. INTRODUCTION: GETTING ACQUAINTED AND SETTING OBJECTIVES

  II. MINI-LECTURE: WHAT IS STRESS?

  III. EXERCISE AND MINI-LECTURE: GOOD AND BAD STRESS; DISEASES OF STRESS

  IV. MINI-LECTURE: DISEASES OF THE TWENTIETH CENTURY

  V. EXERCISE: RECOGNIZING STRESS IN OURSELVES

    (Lunch)

  VI. EXERCISE: WAYS WE EXPRESS STRESS

  VII. MINI-LECTURE: MATCHING STRESS MANAGEMENT METHODS WITH TYPES OF STRESS

  VIII. MINI-LECTURE AND PRACTICE OF DEEP MUSCLE RELAXATION

  IX. MINI-LECTURE AND PRACTICE OF THE RELAXATION RESPONSE (MEDITATION)

  X. MINI-LECTURE: OTHER STRESS MANAGEMENT TECHNIQUES AND PRINCIPLES

  XI. SUMMING UP AND EVALUATION OF WORKSHOP

I. INTRODUCTION: GETTING ACQUAINTED AND SETTING OBJECTIVES

Fill Out Name Tags

Ask participants to fill out name tags as they arrive and answer the following questions briefly.

- What is your definition of stress?

- In what ways do you cope with stress?

- What are your goals for the workshop?

Introduce Yourself

Include your name, position, title; perhaps mention any formal or special training and background that are relevant to leading a workshop on stress management. Describe how you will be handling the role of leader: structuring activities, and being a facilitator and resource person.

Purpose of Workshop

State the following in your own words: "This workshop is designed to help you learn to cope more effectively with stress. In this technologically advanced society we are all affected by stress, no matter what our age. Every day each of us has to adapt to unexpected change—just getting to work some days can be a significant source of stress. In relationships between the sexes, men and women have no guidelines to follow. Religion no longer provides the answers. Uncertainty and change are the norm; just to survive requires mental vigilance and constant adaptation. The price we pay is in stress and in stress-related disease.

"Most of you probably know something about stress, especially about some of the harmful effects such as high blood pressure, tension headaches, and insomnia. But few people understand fully what stress is, and how to prevent or alleviate some of these harmful effects.

"There are three major goals for this workshop:

- To help you understand what stress is,

- To help you recognize sources of stress in your life,

- To provide an opportunity to learn and practice effective stress-management techniques, with an emphasis on deep muscle relaxation.

91

"After you complete this workshop you will have a beginning knowledge of stress, which you can utilize to design your own personal stress-management program."

Overview of Workshop
Briefly review the day's agenda, listed where everyone can see it.

Setting Objectives
"At this point I'd like you to meet one another and find out what others hope to gain from today's experience. To accomplish this with a large crowd we will use an exercise called Party Mix. Each of you filled out a name tag and listed three items:

• Your definition of stress

• Ways you cope with stress

• Your goals for the workshop

"I'd like everyone to stand up now. Mill around silently and read as many name tags as you can while others are reading yours. When I say stop, form a group with two people you don't know, then sit down with your group." (Allow 5 minutes, then call "stop.")

"Now that you are in triads, please count off 1, 2, 3. Person 1 will begin by talking for one minute about any aspects of his or her name tag. When I call time, switch to person 2. Person 2 then has one minute to talk, then person 3."

II. MINI-LECTURE: WHAT IS STRESS?

"Let's begin by finding out what you know already about identifying stress. I will read you a list of situations and ask you to raise your hand if you would call any stressful.

• You just changed to a better job.

• You've been unemployed for over six months.

• You just celebrated your 40th birthday.

• You were awarded ten points on the Gong Show.

- You had your first grandchild.

- You're finally taking that vacation you've looked forward to all year.

- You've recently received a promotion.

- You scraped a fender on your new car.

- You slipped on the ice and sprained your ankle.

- Your dentist says you'll need some major work done on your teeth.

- Your town has just been hit by a major snowstorm.

- You and your lover share a passionate kiss.

"As you can see from everyone's responses, whether something is stressful seems to depend on how you see it—and this is correct, as you'll find out when we look at what is known about stress.

"The word 'stress' is a frequently used word that is not understood well. We will often say of someone who is ill or having any kind of problem in life that he or she is 'under a lot of stress.' When we can't identify the cause of physical or emotional difficulties, we are likely to say, 'It's all due to stress.' There may be more truth in this than we realize, but it doesn't solve the problem or cure the ailment if we stop there and don't understand better what stress is all about. The growing interest in stress and in courses and workshops such as this one reflects the growing awareness of the general public that stress is related to many physical and mental disorders.

"We will begin by defining stress and the components of stress so that you can understand it more fully. This understanding can lead to uncovering ways to control stress instead of having it control you. We will then identify some of the sources of stress in our daily lives and learn some effective ways for dealing with them.

"A growing body of knowledge about stress has been accumulating over the past forty years, ever since Dr. Hans Selye first developed a theory of stress. Dr. Selye has spent most of his life conducting research on stress, and he now heads the International Institute of Stress at the University of Montreal. Many other physicians and psychologists are conducting research on stress that is contributing to our understanding and developing some promising methods of stress management. The stress researchers are beginning to provide insights into how the mind and body work together to produce psychosomatic illness and how this knowledge can be used for prevention."

Definition of Stress: The General Adaptation Syndrome (G.A.S.)
"One definition used by Hans Selye is 'the rate of wear and tear within the body'; another, the more precise medical definition Dr. Selye developed as a result of his research, we need to look at in order to understand stress and how to manage it. 'Stress is the body's nonspecific response to any demand placed on it, whether or not that demand is pleasant.' This means the body reacts to stress in the same way regardless of the source of the stress. The body has a three-stage reaction to stress:

• The alarm reaction

• Resistance

• Exhaustion

"This three-stage response is called the General Adaptation Syndrome, or G.A.S.

"In the alarm stage, the body recognizes the stressor, such as an attacking dog, and prepares for fight or flight. The body does this by sending messages from the brain (hypothalamus), which stimulate the pituitary to release its hormones. These trigger the adrenal glands to pour out adrenaline. Adrenaline increases heartbeat and rate of breathing, raises blood sugar level, increases perspiration, dilates the pupils, and slows digestion. The process results in a huge burst of energy, greater muscular strength, and better hearing and vision—all abilities that you can use to fight or flee.

"In the resistance stage, the body repairs any damage caused by the stress and may adapt or get used to such stresses as extreme cold, hard physical labor, worries. However, if the stress continues the body must remain alert and can't repair the damage, leading to the stage of exhaustion. If exhaustion continues, you can develop one of the diseases of stress such as high blood pressure, arteriosclerosis, migraine headaches, gastrointestinal disorders, rheumatoid arthritis, or asthma. The body may give up during this stage and die.

"Most physical or emotional stressors don't last long and produce changes in us resulting from the first and second stages. At first, we get used to stress. During our lifetime we go through these two stages many times; we need these response mechanisms to adapt to the many demands of living.

"Exhaustion usually affects only parts of the body: runners in the Boston Marathon experience severe stress in their muscles and cardiovascular system, which leads to exhaustion, but after a good rest they are back to normal and are looking forward to the next race."

III. EXERCISE AND MINI-LECTURE: GOOD AND BAD STRESS

"Let's take a few minutes now to find out what kinds of activities or situations you experience as good stress and bad stress.

"First, will everyone please stand up, find two other people you'd like to meet, and sit down in groups of three. Count off 1, 2, 3. Now will everyone think of three stressors you encounter frequently that are good for you and three that are bad. Write them on these cards. (Pass out 3 x 5" cards with pencils. Allow about 2 minutes for people to do this.)

"Now, will all the 3's share with your partners for one minute what makes these situations particularly stressful for you. Then the 1's, then the 2's. Now spend five minutes giving each other feedback; be alert to any similarities or discoveries in your group."

After the exercise, reassemble the whole group and have members discuss what they learned or discovered.

Types of Stress

"By now you might be wondering, is all stress bad? A life without stress would be boring and we'd be cabbages. Selye says it can be the spice of life. It's impossible to live without experiencing some degree of stress all the time. Even when we are asleep our bodies are functioning; dreaming produces some stress. We would have to be dead to be free of all stress. Looking back at the list of situations you voted on, each item is potentially stressful. However, some might be considered bad stressors that can cause damage or distress and others are obviously pleasurable. When you embrace your lover you feel your pulse race, your breathing speed up, and your heart pound. Would you want to give up this pleasure? Most of the other situations are subject to your own interpretations. Not everyone perceives the same situation in the same way, so what is stressful for me may not be stressful for you.

"A key idea Selye presents is that 'what matters is not so much what happens to us, but the way we take it.' Herein lies the key to stress management and a concept that relates to psychosomatic medicine. We will make use of this important principle in the afternoon, when we will introduce you to some techniques for reducing the stress reaction.

"Selye says that a certain amount of stress is needed for well-being and is good for us. He calls this positive stress. The G.A.S. can stimulate us enough so we can achieve peak performances for important jobs. You can probably recall times when you 'came through' despite minor illness or low energy. We hear of people performing amazing feats of strength at times of emergency—such as lifting cars. Other examples of adaptation to stress: a date with someone new; an infant learning to walk; a student facing an exam; a job interview. We grow excited and tense while watching our favorite team in a play-off match. Pleasurable emotions produce feelings of exhilaration. These positive stresses put less demand on the body than do negative stresses, for reasons not yet understood. They energize us and produce healthy relaxation.

"The kind of stress that can be harmful Dr. Selye calls 'distress.' Distress results when the stress continues so that we need to keep adapting to it. If the distress continues long enough, it can result in exhaustion. Here are some examples:

• A boring job

• Serious illness of self or family member

• Lack of sleep

• Relationship problems with spouse, family, friends

• Worries about money, family

• Bottled-up feelings such as intense anger, fears, frustrations

"Long-term distress can contribute to the development of migraine headaches, peptic ulcers, heart attacks, hypertension, mental illness, and suicide."

"Most of the stressors we encounter are emotional stressors. The stressor effect depends more on how we react to the stress and less on what caused it. Each of us has developed ways of reacting to the various stressors we encounter. It is this conditioned response that can create problems and possible threats to our health. It can help us learn how to manage stress if we first identify some of the common stressors most of us have to deal with at some time."

Following is a chart describing types of stress. You might present this material as a brief lecture and ask the group to give examples. Another option that works well is to form four groups of 3 to 5 people, and ask each to compile a list of stressors for one of the four categories: life-cycle stressors, social stress, physical and personal stress, and job stress. Allow 5 minutes. Ask each group to read its list and write it out on a flipchart or chalkboard. After all groups have reported, ask the group for additions that were overlooked. Add any from the following chart that have not been mentioned. The purpose of this exercise is to emphasize the broad range of stressors everyone experiences throughout the life span.

TYPES OF STRESS

Life-Cycle Stressors

Infancy	frustration of needs for care, to be played with, talked to, cuddled.
Childhood	tasks of physical and emotional development: stress of meeting the demands of developing independence from parents and in relationships with brothers, sisters, teachers, other children.
Adolescence	relationships with the opposite sex; friendships; job and career decisions, worries; school pressures and decisions.
Early marriage	
Pregnancy	
Parenthood	demands of filling new roles, readjusting relationships, making major changes in the way your time is spent.
Divorce	
Single parenting	
Job change	
Middle years	death of spouse, children leaving home, restlessness with your present life and work.
Senior years	devaluation by society, retirement, health problems, reduced income, death of friends and family, transfers to homes for the aged.

Social Stress

Economic instability	inflation, recession.
Unemployment	
Urban living	overcrowding, noise, traffic jams, pollution, crime, poor housing, inadequate schools.

Changing values   women's liberation movement, changing male/female roles and relationships, sexual attitude and behavior change, children's differing values and mores.

Relocation

Travel

Physical Stress

Illness

Accidental injury

Substance use   coffee, alcohol, soft drinks, medication, illegal drugs.

Personal Stress

Attitudes about oneself

Expectations of others

Feelings

These personal stress factors determine whether we view a particular event as stressful and if so, how stressful.

Job Stress

Conflict with coworkers

Job dissatisfaction

Overwork

Lack of support

Unclear job expectations

Time pressure

Monotonous work

Unchallenging work

Job stress is universal and intense, and is experienced by nearly everyone.

IV. MINI-LECTURE: DISEASES OF THE TWENTIETH CENTURY

"The science of medicine has conquered many of the major infectious diseases that were fatal in the past for huge numbers of people. Sometimes, entire communities were wiped out. In the western countries we've witnessed the disappearance of such diseases as cholera, typhoid, smallpox, and, more recently, diptheria, whooping cough, measles, and polio. Our success in eradicating these diseases results from high-level medical technology and research. Medical researchers have been able to study the causes of these diseases—the germs and viruses that make us sick—and discover methods to destroy the microorganisms involved.

"At the same time, we are experiencing an enormous increase in deaths from diseases that are related to psychological and environmental factors. These are the stress-related disorders—the major diseases of modern twentieth-century society: cardiovascular disorders, cancer, arthritis, respiratory disease. These diseases are not conquered easily, because the causes are extremely complex. They are not due to a single germ or virus for which we can develop an antitoxin. Researchers will be struggling for many years to identify their causes.

"Our ability to cope with these diseases as a society and as individuals is hampered by our attitudes and beliefs about why we get sick. The way we react to our own illnesses, and the way we are treated by others when we get sick, including many of our physicians, is to assume that something outside of us made us sick. To get well again we need only to take the proper medicine, allow ourselves to receive proper care, and give up our personal and social responsibilities until the disease-causing factors are vanquished. This is essentially a passive approach to regaining health. It is how we respond when germs are the culprits—we view ourselves as victims, powerless without the skill of the physician. We hold these beliefs and adopt the role of victim to our own detriment when faced with stress-related disorders.

"Long-held beliefs are not given up easily—especially when we have such a wondrous, miracle-producing medical technology at our command. Our health insurance system perpetuates the attitude of individual helplessness and dependence on the physician *after* we have succumbed to illness. Reimbursement is limited to disease care; we cannot collect payment for preventive services. If insurance payments were available for participating in educational programs, this would be a powerful incentive for individuals to take active responsibility in their own health care and for health-care providers to develop effective educational programs.

"In contrast to our beliefs about disease, we tend to hold the individual responsible for mental illness. Psychiatrists help people look at what they might be doing or thinking that could contribute to the onset of maintenance of emotional problems. The mentally ill usually don't receive the empathy and nurturance people lavish on the physically ill. Greeting cards to cheer the mentally ill have never been developed!

"Consciously and unconsciously, we've learned that it's socially acceptable to be physically ill because of the generally accepted belief that we can't help it. For some people, the benefits of illness become so attractive that unconsciously we program our body to make us sick or to prolong or inhibit our recuperation. Perhaps as a child you discovered you could stay home from school or avoid facing up to some event you wished would go away if you had a stomachache—your mind and body learned how to work together to bring on an actual upset stomach.

"Researchers are learning more about the factors that lead to stress disease and have identified the following:

• When stress continues unabated or is extreme, it becomes excessive stress.

• Changes in the nervous system and the body organs, including reduction of white cells and suppression of the immune system, create conditions for disease.

• A high concentration of life-change events can contribute to disease.

When this combination of factors occurs, there is a likelihood that disease will develop.

"Researchers have been looking into the possibility that there may be a link between a specific personality style, emotions, and the onset of a particular kind of stress disease. There is no question that personality influences the way we react to stress. In childhood, we learn through trial and error how to deal with stressful situations. And we learn by watching parents, teachers, and other people. Our past successes, failures, rewards, and punishments may still be determining how we handle stress now in our daily life. If we are lucky, our learned perceptions of stress and responses to it are still functional and effective. But most of us have not had the good fortune to learn in childhood, when the stresses were different, how to manage the stress we face as adults.

"Some individuals, sometimes without realizing it, have developed personality styles and defenses that may contribute to stress disease. We may feel so fearful of making mistakes, of being criticized, of doing less than a perfect job, that we withdraw from challenging situations or avoid confrontations. We may then feel unfulfilled, frustrated, incompetent. As children, we may have learned that expressing feelings—especially anger—can get us into trouble. Instead of being open and honest about how we feel, we express our anger indirectly or deny it altogether. We may develop headaches or stomachaches. We may suppress our need for caring and affection by doing for others—a much-loved ploy of teachers and other helping professionals.

"The largest body of evidence linking style of response to stress with a specific disease is the research begun by Meyer Friedman and Ray Rosenman,[1] two cardiologists who first described Type A behavior and concluded that this behavior pattern is a major cause of coronary heart disease. Type A behavior pattern they found to be more predictive of coronary heart disease than the standard risk factors. They wrote a book about it—*Type A Behavior and Your Heart*—which describes the behavior and offers suggestions for modifying behavior to avoid a heart attack.

"Researchers are learning more about the factors that lead to stress disease and have identified the following:

"Type A behavior is characterized by a competitive, aggressive, achievement-oriented, time-dominated orientation to life. Type A people are usually unaware that their behavior creates problems for others or is detrimental to their health and well-being, since this behavior is condoned and applauded by our achievement-oriented society.

"Type A men and women share two common traits:

- excessive competitive drive, which is present in all areas of their life—they have a drive to excel in everything they do;

- chronic time urgency—they are continually driven by the clock, by having to meet deadlines; they are obsessed by numbers; they try to do more and more at a faster and faster pace; they are running on an accelerating treadmill of their own making.

"Many Type A's also exhibit free-floating hostility, especially toward other competitors—usually other Type A's or people and situations that slow them down. A slow driver poking along in front of him or her can arouse a Type A's hostility to a fever pitch.

---

[1] Meyer Friedman, M.D. and Ray H. Rosenman, M.D. *Type A Behavior and Your Heart.* New York: Fawcett Crest Books, 1974.

"Type A's can't relax and do nothing. Weekends, vacations, free time with family and friends can't be enjoyed, because the Type A—obsessed by work and the need to achieve and accumulate things—is busy worrying about the time spent being nonproductive. Type A's will not allow themselves the leisure to develop hobbies or new interests. They have developed a manner of talking—which is usually much of the time—that reveals how driven they are: they finish sentences for others, interrupt often, hurry them along. To make a point Type A's raise their voices and talk louder and faster. They are not good listeners, and are less aware of others. They often demonstrate impatience and hostility.

"Underlying this angry, driven life-style is a basic feeling of insecurity that is aroused if the Type A fails to have full control over the people and events in his or her life. Type A's have trouble coping with the novel and unexpected; they are more seriously affected by losses in their lives than Type B's. Type A's are engaged in a chronic struggle with life, keeping their arteries and entire body in overdrive to meet the threats that never end.

"The behavior of a Type B person, in constrast, is everything Type A's cannot allow themselves to be. Type B's have found a comfortable, more relaxed cruising speed at which to travel through life. They look at the scenery with enjoyment, allow time for frequent refreshment and rest stops, really enjoy being alone or with friends and family. Type B's work more slowly and thoughtfully, which can permit greater creativity. They allow themselves the leisure to develop more fully as people, and to have a number of interests, activities, and friendships outside of work. Many Type B's have plenty of drive—some are heads of corporations—but time is scheduled with a calendar, not a stopwatch. Type B's have learned how to enjoy life.

"Most people do not have all the characteristics of the Type A pattern at all times, but if you recognize any of them in yourself or suspect that you are moving in that direction you should consider modifying your life-style. Friedman and Roseman have many specific suggestions for changing Type A behavior.

"With regard to the other stress-related diseases such as cancer, arthritis, asthma, ulcers, and migraine headaches, the research connecting personality factors with these diseases is still inconclusive. There is an urgent need to study what relationship exists between personality factors and illness. The underlying causes of any specific disease are extremely complex, and will

102

probably always be composed of an array of physical, emotional, and environmental components.

"Perhaps most important, the assessment of your individual risk factors needs to be conducted and evaluated by a skilled clinician, because the average person lacks the experience and knowledge to make such a judgment. However, by increasing your awareness of accumulating evidence—though still imprecise—that many factors contribute to the common diseases of modern society, you can begin taking preventive action before symptoms develop. You might decide to consult with your physician to help you evaluate and modify your life-style and improve your general health in order to minimize the effects of stress in your life and reduce the risks of stress-related disease."

V. EXERCISE: RECOGNIZING STRESS IN OURSELVES

Introduction
"To reduce stress in your life, you can begin by making a personal assessment of the sources of stress and how you respond to these stresses. Each of us reacts differently to stress depending on our life circumstances, our personality, the patterns of behavior we have developed, and our physical characteristics. We need to understand our own style of response to stress. With a little self-study, each of us can find some attitudes and responses that are creating distress and discover some ways to modify them so that stress is less destructive to us.

"As you consider the stresses in your life, keep in mind that we are continually adapting to stressors, both positive and negative, and that excessive stress may lead to illness or poor health. Learning to recognize when stress levels are becoming too high and our health is in danger can tell us when to take preventive action."

Exercise
Give each participant a copy of the Handout, "How Much Stress Is In Your Life?"

"To begin increasing your awareness about the sources of stress in your life, we will use a brief questionnaire developed by Dr. Thomas Holmes.

"Dr. Holmes, a pioneering researcher in the field of stress-related illnesses at the University of Washington in Seattle, has designed a written test to help you predict your chances of getting sick in the near future in relation to the amount of stress in your life.

"Score yourself on his Life Change Test. Check only those events that you have experienced in the past year.

"This should take about 10 minutes. Then, in groups of three, share your reactions to the questionnaire, including any ideas you have about coping better with stress."

(Note to Leader: You may want to break for lunch at this point.)

VI. EXERCISE: WAYS WE EXPRESS STRESS

Introduction
"Is there any way that each of us can tell whether we have experienced more stress than our bodies can handle? Dr. Hans Selye has identified a list of symptoms and behaviors that are pretty reliable indicators that we are suffering from distress. This list of danger signs is not meant to increase stress by raising our anxiety level about our state of health, but to serve as a signal to take some preventive action. Instead of waiting to become sick, we can learn to recognize signs of severe stress and take steps to remove the source of stress or reduce the stress reaction. In this way we can take active responsibility for our health and prevent many stress-related illnesses."

Exercise
Give each participant a copy of the Handout, "Self-observable Signs of Stress Stress."

"Now let's look at Selye's list. Check off the ways you express stress. You will be doing this for your own information only. You might want to circle the reaction to stress that gives you the most difficulty or the one that occurs most often."

Allow about 5 minutes for participants to do this.

VII. MINI-LECTURE: MATCHING STRESS MANAGEMENT METHODS WITH TYPE OF STRESS

"Individuals vary in how they respond to the tension of daily life. We mentioned before that what is stressful for one person may not distress another. Further, people do not respond to stress in the same ways.

"Some of us express stress physically; we may develop headaches, hypertension, or ulcers. Others have trouble concentrating, feel their mind racing, or experience emotional reactions such as increased anxiety or fearfulness, depression, or obsessive negative thoughts. One way to counteract the effects of stress is through relaxation. Edmund Jacobson, developer of Deep Muscle Relaxation, sums it up as follows:

> 'Anxiety and tension are imcompatible with physical
> and mental relaxation. If a person lets himself relax,
> he can control or block the anxiety, tension, or fears.'[1]

"Certain methods work best to reduce bodily stress symptoms while others combat mental and emotional stress symptoms. The basic principles to guide us in choosing the best methods for us are:

• Self-regulation of behavior (including voluntary focusing of attention) in a given mode (physical or mental) to reduce or inhibit unwanted activity in that specific mode.

• Self-regulation of behavior in a given mode (physical or mental) may, to a lesser degree, reduce unwanted activity in other modes.[2]

"In other words, one needs to identify how one responds to stress (physically or mentally or both) and then pick a method that works directly on that mode. Procedures that affect bodily tension directly reduce physical stress most effectively; techniques that result in changes in mental events are most effective with mental and emotional stress."

Pass out the "Types of Stress . . . " Handout so that participants can jot down notes while you talk.

---

[1] Edmund Jacobson, *Progressive Relaxation.* Chicago: University of Chicago, 1929.

[2] From "Matching Relaxation Therapies to Types of Anxiety: A Patterning Approach," by Richard J. Davidson and Gary E. Schwartz, in *Relax: How You Can Feel Better and Reduce Stress and Overcome Tension,* edited by John White and James Fadiman. The Confucian Press, 1976, p. 191.

105

Types of Stress and Suggested Relaxation Techniques for Each
"I would like each of you to close your eyes and recall the last time you felt distressed. Try to recall how you reacted to that stress. Decide if it was primarily a physical or mental reaction. Many of us, when under intense stress, react both physically and mentally, but most of us favor one mode or the other. When you have a good idea of your usual mode of expression, open your eyes.

"I am going to review three modes of reacting to stress and describe some methods that work well for each mode. Be thinking about which method might suit your needs."

A. "**Techniques for those who suffer physical symptoms** (headaches, backaches, stiff necks, tense or rigid body, ulcers, high blood pressure, etc.)

• "Deep Muscle Relaxation (D.M.R.): Developed by Dr. Edmund Jacobson, D.M.R. is especially good for high somatic and low cognitive stress. This is a passive process which involves focusing attention on the various gross muscle groups throughout the body. First you tense, then release each group of muscles while thinking, 'relax, relax, relax,' to build up an association between mental process and physical relaxation. Practicing D.M.R. builds up somatic cues so that eventually an automatic relaxation response will take place when one thinks, 'relax.'

• "Progressive Relaxation: This is a similar technique, except that you do not tense your muscles. Instead, you mentally suggest relaxation by thinking words like, 'my feet are completely relaxed, my feet are completely relaxed,' while consciously relaxing those muscles. This is often accompanied by deep breathing or visualization techniques, and may be used as a warmup exercise to systematic desensitization, which I will describe in a few minutes.

• "Autogenic Training: Developed by Dr. J. H. Schultz, this passive somatic attention technique involves leaning back in a comfortable chair in a quiet room. With eyes closed, you use verbal formulas to make mental contact with parts of your body. For example, you might say to yourself, 'my arm is getting warm and heavy'; you will then feel relaxed with a warm, heavy arm. There are a series of steps to learn in order to use this method effectively. Essentially it involves meditating about a somatic event in order to produce somatic change.

• "Hatha Yoga: This ancient system of self-development leads to physical and mental calmness and is good for controlling moderate somatic and

106

cognitive stress. It includes physical exercises and relaxation as well as breathing techniques, nutrition, and concentration.

- "Massage: Active somatic techniques can help you achieve a good balance between relaxation and stimulation, rest and activity. Self-massage can improve posture and circulation, and make you aware of the tensions and stresses that build up in your body over the day. Massage directly relaxes muscle tension.

- "Deep Breathing Exercises: When you breathe softly and slowly, it is difficult for your emotions to become aroused out of a tranquil state. Deep breathing can reduce tension by producing a deep state of calmness and relaxation. Several disciplines include breathing exercises as part of their relaxation strategies. In yoga, 'Pranayama,' or control of the life force, is an important study. Since we all must breathe anyway, breath control is a quick and simple way to relieve tension and increase energy.

- "Exercise: Unlike machines that wear out from overuse, our bodies are made for activity. Long life and health are promoted by regular exercise of the body. If we don't exercise, we tend to atrophy. We become more susceptible to disease and less able to combat stress."

B. **"Techniques for those who suffer mental symptoms** (worry, obsessive thoughts, mind racing, inability to concentrate, etc.)

- "Meditation—The Relaxation Response: This technique, developed by Dr. Herbert Benson, works best on low cognitive and somatic stress and is especially useful for people with borderline hypertension. It involves regulating your attention to produce a state of general autonomic quiescence. If attention is focused on a mantra or scene, it will reduce stress more effectively than if attention is focused on a bodily process such as breathing.

- "Hatha Yoga: Hatha Yoga promotes mental and spiritual pacification. Relaxation, deep breathing exercises, and concentration all aim to reduce tension, overcome fear, and produce feelings of inner peace and tranquility.

- "Deep Breathing with Visualization: When a pleasant scene or image is conjured up while relaxing through deep breathing, the visualization blocks other mental activity and reduces stress.

- "Progressive Relaxation with Mental Focus and Visualization: Focusing on the words 'calm' and 'relaxed' while breathing deeply—'calm' on inhale and 'relaxed' on exhale—or visualizing a relaxing scene (lying on a beach, etc.) can produce mental relaxation.

- "Active Generation of Cognitive Behavior: Distracting your mind from worry or distress by focusing on a mentally demanding game or other activity can reduce mental stress.

- "Involvement of Entire Perceptual-Cognitive System: Watching TV or a movie, or reading a book, which we commonly refer to as 'escape' activities, are ways of diverting attention from adverse stimuli and resting the mind.

- "Activities: Dancing, walking, and sports involve us mentally and physically and can relieve stress by diverting attention from our problems while maintaining our physical health.

- "Systematic Desensitization: This set of procedures is designed to treat problems associated with inappropriate conditioned anxiety. The steps involve a) deep muscle relaxation; b) establishing a scale of subjective anxiety responses; c) constructing a hierarchy of anxiety-provoking stimuli; and, d) simultaneously maintaining the relaxed state and imagining anxiety-associated stimuli from the hierarchy. This procedure enables people to learn a new response to a stimuli that previously was associated with fear. It is especially useful for specific phobias, performance anxiety, and other problems of malconditioning.

- "Hypnosis: This active cognitive process attempts to reduce anxiety by the active generation of mental behavior. It involves shifting attention and generating imagery (for example, 'imagine you are holding something heavy in your hand').

C. "Techniques for a combination of physical and mental stresses

- "Vigorous Physical Exercise: This demands active physical and mental attention and, therefore, reduces both modes of stress. Tennis, jogging, biking, hiking, swimming, martial arts, sports such as basketball and volleyball—all demand physical and mental involvement that preclude symptoms from appearing at the same time."

VIII. MINI-LECTURE AND PRACTICE OF DEEP MUSCLE RELAXA-TION

"Deep Muscle Relaxation, or D.M.R., is the most widely used technique to help people counteract and control bodily stress. For those of us who suffer migraine or tension headaches, ulcers, backaches, hypertension, stiff necks, or tenseness elsewhere in our bodies (often set off by sitting at a desk in one position all day or from underuse of our bodies), D.M.R. can be a very helpful way to control stress.

"In the modern world, people need to counteract some of their innate biological coping mechanisms in order to relax. The 'fight or flight' response helped ancient man to survive, but today it is often counterproductive. The spurt of adrenaline, bracing of neck and back muscles, and quickened pulse that accompany sudden fear or anxiety usually have no appropriate physical outlet: it is socially unacceptable, for example, to run out of the boss's office or to strike him when we're upset, so we maintain an outward appearance of calm while clenching our teeth and suppressing our rage or fear. Because we are constantly exposed to stimuli that set off this survival reaction, we often feel tensed for flight or fight. The physical reaction we feel, when chronic, can lead to headaches, backaches, or other physical illnesses that are much more serious.

"Unfortunately, many people use drugs, alcohol, or food to seek relief from this constant stress. We have become a nation of pill poppers, constantly faced with ads promising relief of backache or headache with pills or tranquilizers. Reliance on drugs is expensive, risky to our bodies, and can end up in addiction. D.M.R. is an alternative that will help you counteract the effects of bodily stress.

"D.M.R. was developed back in the 1930s by Dr. Edmund Jacobson, a clinical psychologist, who discovered that people can regulate certain effects of the autonomic nervous system through self-management techniques. In other words, one can achieve control over one's skeletal muscles and reduce levels of tension in those muscles. When we are keyed up by our biologic coping responses, we can, after practicing, consciously instruct our muscle fibers to relax. When muscle fibers are lengthened (in a state of relaxation), they cannot at the same time express tension; they cannot contract as they do in a fight or flight response. Anxiety and muscular relaxation produce opposite physiologic states, so one cannot be anxious when completely relaxed.

"Jacobson's technique simply involves learning to tighten and then relax the major muscles of the body. Practicing this daily teaches you to recognize what muscular tension feels like (the tensing) and to relax each muscle group in order to achieve total relaxation. After regular practice, you can voluntarily relax muscle groups at will when you notice tenseness developing."

Practice of D.M.R.
Read the following script and explain that a summary handout will be given out later so that participants can practice at home.

Suggest that people practice while sitting in a chair. If they lie down, they may fall asleep, which is not the purpose of the exercise. The purpose is to teach people to make a conscious effort to relax. With practice they will learn to relax tense muscles while doing their daily activities.

If people eventually do want to do the exercise lying down, mention that to avoid stress to the lower back they should bend their knees. Anyone with lower back problems should consult a doctor before doing the part of the exercise that involves arching the lower back.

Relaxation Script[1]
"Arms: Settle back as comfortably as you can. Let yourself relax to the best of your ability. Now, as you relax like that, clench your right fist. Just clench your fist tighter and tighter, and study the tension as you do so. Keep it clenched and feel the tension in your right fist, hand, forearm. Now relax. Let the fingers of your right hand become loose, and observe the contrast in your feelings.

"Now, let yourself go and try to become more relaxed all over. Once more, clench your right fist really tight. Hold it, and notice the tension again. Now let go, relax; your fingers straighten out, and you notice the difference once more.

"Now repeat this with your left fist. Clench your left fist while the rest of your body relaxes; clench that fist tighter and feel the tension. And now relax. Again enjoy the contrast. Repeat that once more: clench the left fist,

---

[1] Reprinted from *Behavior Therapy Techniques: A Guide to the Treatment of Neuroses* by Joseph Wolpe and Arnold A. Lazarus. Oxford, England: Pergamon Press, Ltd. Used with permission of the publisher.

110

tight and tense. Now do the opposite of tension: relax and feel the difference. Continue relaxing like that for a while.

"Clench both fists tighter and tighter: both fists tense, forearms tense. Study the sensations. Relax. Straighten out your fingers and feel that relaxation. Continue relaxing your hands and forearms more and more.

"Now bend your elbows and tense your biceps; tense them harder and study the tension feelings. All right, straighten out your arms; let them relax and feel that difference again. Let the relaxation develop. Once more, tense your biceps; hold the tension and observe it carefully. Straighten the arms and relax; relax to the best of your ability. Each time, pay close attention to your feelings when you tense up and relax. Now straighten your arms; straighten them so that you feel the most tension in the triceps muscles along the back of your arms; stretch your arms and feel that tension. Now relax.

"Get your arms back into a comfortable position. Let the relaxation proceed on its own. The arms should feel comfortably heavy as you allow them to relax. Straighten the arms once more so that you feel the tension in the triceps muscles; straighten them. Feel that tension, and relax.

"Now let's concentrate on pure relaxation in the arms without any tension. Get your arms comfortable and let them relax further and further. Continue relaxing your arms even further. Even when your arms seem fully relaxed, try to go that extra bit further; try to achieve still deeper levels of relaxation.

"Face, Neck, Shoulders, Upper Back: Let all your muscles go loose and heavy. Just settle back quietly and comfortably. Wrinkle up your forehead; relax and smooth it out. Picture the entire forehead and scalp becoming smoother as the relaxation increases. Now frown and crease your brows and study the tension; let go of the tension again. Smooth out the forehead once more.

"Now, close your eyes tighter and tighter. Feel the tension, and relax your eyes. Keep your eyes closed, gently, comfortably, and notice the relaxation. Now clench your jaws, bite your teeth together; study the tension throughout the jaws; relax your jaws now. Let your lips part slightly. Appreciate the relaxation. Now press your tongue hard against the roof of your mouth. Look for the tension. All right, let your tongue return to a comfortable and relaxed position. Now purse your lips. Press your lips together tighter and tighter; relax them. Note the contrast between the tension and your relaxation. Feel the relaxation all over your face, all over your forehead

111

and scalp, eyes, jaws, lips, tongue, and throat. The relaxation progresses further and further.

"Now attend to your neck muscles. Press your head back as far as it can go and feel the tension in the neck; roll it to the right and feel the tension shift; now roll it to the left. Straighten your head and bring it forward; press your chin against your chest. Let your head return to a comfortable position, and study the relaxation. Let the relaxation develop. Feels good? Now shrug your shoulders, as tight as they will go. Hold the tension. Feel the pain. Drop your shoulders and feel the relaxation. Your neck and shoulders are relaxed. Shrug your shoulders again and move them around, loosely, easily, relaxed.

"Bring your shoulders up and forward and back. Feel the tension in your shoulders and in your upper back. Drop the shoulders once more, and relax. Pause to think; let the relaxation spread deep into the shoulders, right into your back muscles. Feel a wave of peace spread through them. Let the relaxation spread deep into the shoulders, right into your back muscles. Relax your neck and throat and your jaws and the rest of your face. The pure relaxation takes over and grows deeper, deeper, ever deeper.

"Chest, Stomach, Lower Back: Relax your entire body to the best of your ability. Feel that comfortable heaviness that comes with relaxation. Breathe easily and freely, in and out. Notice how the relaxation increases as you exhale; as you breathe out, just feel the relaxation. Now breathe right in and fill your lungs; inhale deeply and hold your breath. Study the tension. Now exhale. Let the walls of your chest grow loose and push the air out automatically. Continue relaxing and breathe freely and gently. Feel the relaxation and enjoy it. With the rest of your body as relaxed as possible, fill your lungs again. Breathe in deeply and hold it again. Fine. Let the air out and appreciate the relief. Just breathe normally. Continue relaxing your chest and let the relaxation spread to your back, shoulders, neck, and arms. Merely let go, and enjoy the relaxation.

"Now let's attend to your stomach area. Tighten your stomach muscles; make your abdomen hard. Notice the tension, then relax. Let the muscles loosen and notice the contrast. Once more, press and tighten your stomach muscles. Hold the tension and study it, then relax. Notice the general well-being that comes with relaxing your stomach. Now draw your stomach in. Pull the muscles right in and feel the tension this way; now relax again. Let your stomach out. Continue breathing normally and easily and feel the gentle massaging action all over your chest and stomach. Again pull your stomach in and hold the tension. Now push out and tense like that. Hold the tension. Once more pull in and feel the tension; now relax your stomach fully. Let the tension dissolve as the relaxation grows deeper. Each time you breathe out, notice the rhythmic relaxation both in your lungs and in your stomach. Notice how your chest and your stomach relax more and more. Try and let go of all contradictions anywhere in your body.

"Now direct your attention to your lower back. Arch up your back, make your lower back quite hollow, and feel the tension along your spine. Settle down comfortably again, relaxing the lower back. Arch your body up and feel the tension as you do so. Try to keep the rest of your body as relaxed as possible. Try to localize the tension within your lower back area. Relax once more, relaxing further and further. Relax your lower back, relax your upper back, spread the relaxation to your stomach, chest, shoulders, arms, and your face. All these parts relax further, and further, deeper, and even deeper.

"Hips, Thighs, Calves; Complete Body Relaxation: Let go of all tensions and relax. Now flex your buttocks and thighs. Flex your thighs by pressing down on your heels as hard as you can; relax and note the difference. Straighten your knees and flex your thigh muscles again. Hold the tension, then relax your hips and thighs. Allow the relaxation to proceed on its own. Press your feet and toes downward, away from your face, so that your calf muscles become tense. Study that tension; relax your feet and calves. This time, bend your feet toward your face so that you feel tension along your shins. Bring your toes right up; relax again. Keep relaxing for a while. Now let yourself relax further, all over. Relax your feet, ankles, calves and shins, knees, thighs, buttocks, and hips. Feel the heaviness of your lower body as you relax still further.

"Now spread the relaxation to your stomach, waist, lower back. Let go more and more. Feel that relaxation all over. Let it proceed to your upper back, chest, shoulders and arms, and right to the tips of your fingers. Keep relaxing more and more deeply. Make sure that no tension has crept into your throat; relax your neck and your jaws, and all of your facial muscles. Keep relaxing your whole body like that for a while. Let yourself relax.

"Now you can become twice as relaxed as you are, merely by taking in a really deep breath and slowly exhaling. With your eyes closed, so that you become less aware of things around you and thus prevent any surface tensions from developing, breathe in deeply and feel yourself becoming heavier. Take in a long, deep breath and let it out very slowly. Feel how heavy and relaxed you have become.

"In a state of perfect relaxation you should feel unwilling to move a single muscle in your body. Think about the effort that would be required to raise your right arm. As you think about raising your right arm, see if you can notice any tensions that might have crept into your shoulder and your arm. Now you decide not to lift the arm but to continue relaxing. Observe the relief and the disappearance of the tension; just carry on relaxing like that. When you wish to get up, count backward from four to one. You should then feel fine and refreshed, wide awake and calm!"

IX. MINI-LECTURE AND PRACTICE OF THE RELAXATION RESPONSE (MEDITATION)

Introduction
"The Relaxation Response is a simple, mental, nonreligious meditation technique. It is a scientific method of working with the consciousness, which entails concentration of attention and awareness on a single idea, object, or point inside or on the body through repetition of a sound, word, or phrase. The physiological and psychological effects of the relaxation response counteract the body's flight or fight response.

"When practiced systematically for 15 to 20 minutes twice daily, the relaxation response has a significant effect on stress and its side effects. People who meditate regularly have a lowered metabolic rate (blood pressure drops 5 to 10 points, which can reduce borderline hypertension to a normal range); show a marked decrease in the use of alcohol, drugs, and cigarette smoking; show improved ability to deal with stress; and increase their sense of well-being.

"Meditation has also been found to enhance empathy, to sharpen mental processes, and to correlate with various measures of enhanced interpersonal functioning.

"Meditation is not a trance. Awareness is sharpened because you tune in to higher perception. This alteration in consciousness involves a qualitative and quantitative change in mental alertness and visual imagery. These changes in turn produce deep rest and restoration of functioning by interrupting the adverse stimuli that set off the fight or flight response.

"The relaxation response procedure was developed by Dr. Herbert Benson, a Harvard cardiologist who studied the physiological responses to all types

114

of meditation (including Hindu, Buddhist, TM, and Zen) and determined the basic elements necessary to produce relaxation."

Dr. Benson's Relaxation Response Technique

"The basic technique for eliciting the relaxation response is extremely simple. Its elements have been known and used for centuries in many cultures throughout the world.

"Four basic elements are common to all these practices: a quiet environment, a mental device, a passive attitude, and a comfortable position. A simple, mental, noncultic technique based on these four elements follows:

- "A quiet environment: One should choose a quiet, calm environment with as few distractions as possible. Sound, even background noise, may prevent the elicitation of the response. Choose a convenient, suitable place—for example, an office desk in a quiet room.

- "A mental device: The meditator employs the constant stimulus of a single-syllable sound or word. The syllable is repeated silently or in a low, gentle tone. The purpose of the repetition is to free oneself from logical, externally oriented thought by focusing solely on the stimulus. Many different words and sounds have been used in traditional practices. Because of its simplicity and neutrality, the use of the syllable 'one' is suggested.

- "A passive attitude: The purpose of the response is to help one rest and relax, and this requires a completely passive attitude. You should not scrutinize your performance or try to force the response, because this may well prevent the response from occurring. When distracting thoughts enter the mind, they should simply be disregarded.

- "A comfortable position: The meditator should sit in a comfortable chair in as restful a position as possible. The purpose is to reduce muscular effort to a minimum. The head may be supported; the arms should be balanced or supported as well. The shoes may be removed and the feet propped up several inches, if desired. Loosen all tight-fitting clothing."

Practice of Relaxation Response

Read the following script and tell participants they will receive a summary so they can practice at home.

- "In a quiet environment, sit in a comfortable position.

- "Close your eyes.

- "Deeply relax your muscles, beginning at your feet and progressing up to your face: feet, calves, thighs, lower torso, chest, shoulders, neck, head. Allow them to remain deeply relaxed.

- "Breathe through your nose. Become aware of your breathing. As you breathe out, say the word 'one' silently to yourself. Thus: breathe in, breathe out, with 'one.' In, out, with 'one.'

- "Continue this practice for 20 minutes. You may open your eyes to check the time, but do not use an alarm. When you finish, sit quietly for several minutes, first with your eyes closed and then with your eyes open.

"Do not worry about whether you are successful in achieving a deep level of relaxation; maintain a passive attitude and permit relaxation to occur at its own pace. When distracting thoughts occur, ignore them and continue to repeat 'one' as you breathe. The technique should be practiced once or twice daily. Wait at least two hours after any meal, since the digestive processes seem to interfere with the elicitation of the expected changes."

X. MINI-LECTURE: OTHER STRESS MANAGEMENT TECHNIQUES AND PRINCIPLES

Put the following outlines (also included as a Handout) on the board or flipchart and review with participants.

A. Managing Your Time and Energy

Self-Assessment

- "Listen to your body and your feelings for signals of stress.

- "Evaluate your present habits. What price do you pay in terms of stress, discomfort, or lack of enjoyment of life?

- "Be aware of high-stress habits: speaking fast, competing constantly, ignoring or denying tiredness, setting quotas, doing two things at once, pretending to listen, overscheduling, clenching your fists or jaws.

- "Look for stressors—people, places, things—and take responsibility for trying to lower your stress.
- "Find your stress quotient. Ask yourself, Am I taking on too much? If so, slow down your life and your drive."

Planning and Setting Goals

- "Set priorities: choose how to spend your time and energy to balance your life, control your tempo, achieve a healthy balance between work and play, and develop commitment.

- "Schedule time for recreation and hobbies: try to maximize your enjoyment of life. The noise and rush of modern life may keep us in a constantly stimulated state and contribute to a feeling of anxiety. Take a breather, relax, allow yourself time to get places. Take time to enjoy the trip and time to reflect."

B. Improving Your Environment

- "Reduce unnecessary noises and irritations.

- "Get enough rest and sleep in order to be alert and able to cope with stress.

- "Don't use passive, habit-forming ways to blot out stress symptoms—drugs or alcohol—which later cause more stress. These make you dependent on means outside of yourself for control of stress.

- "Anticipate changes and crises; plan how you will deal with stresses—a promotion, a disappointment, for example. Remember that the ability to handle stress comes from within.

- "Improve the way you relate to others. Learn to be more open and honest and to express your feelings and share yourself with others. (Assertiveness training can help here.) Learn to express anger constructively.

- "Build a support system: find security, develop new friendships, ask friends for extra strokes when you need them. Be more open with people, don't criticize or blame others, give in occasionally, do something for others, get involved.

• "Build a comfortable home atmosphere: change your residence, redecorate, put yourself into your physical surroundings and create a comfortable scene around you."

C. Improving Your Internal Environment

• "Develop a positive attitude toward life. Put stressors in a favorable context. If you can convince yourself that some of the stress is useful or necessary, you will reduce the aftereffects of stress. In other words, recognize the beneficial aspects of stress, even to the point of seeking growth lessons in bad experiences. Use the power of positive thinking; your attitude determines whether you perceive any experience as pleasant or unpleasant. People actually control how they choose to see things. Marcus Aurelius said, 'If you are distressed by anything external, the pain is not due to the thing itself but to your estimate of it. This you have the power to revoke at any time.'

• "Learn to take it easy. Many of us take things too seriously and need to take one thing at a time. When we worry too much we need diversion—something to put in the place of worrying—a pleasant thought, thought stoppage (a technique to stop negative thought patterns by shouting words like 'stop' or 'no' in the middle of an anxious series of thoughts), or change of scene (getting away from a painful situation in order to catch your breath and give yourself a new perspective—going to a movie, reading, visiting a friend—doing something to escape from your routine). Remember, 'Worry is like rocking in a rocking chair. It gives you something to do, but gets you nowhere.' (unknown author)

• "Set aside quieting time. Practice the relaxation response or deep muscle relaxation. Regulating the activity of your mind or body will reduce unwanted activity in that mode. Practicing meditation with visualization helps reduce worrying and anxious thoughts and D.M.R. helps reduce tension in the body.

• "Talk out your worries with a friend or a professional (if preoccupied with emotional problems). This helps clarify problems and control anxiety. Therapy, by helping you relax and become aware of your feelings and behavior, helps you remain calm in otherwise anxious situations.

• "Set your goals on inner peace and serenity. We all need to learn to accept what we cannot change, to learn to love ourselves, and not to be afraid. Instead of worrying about the past or the future, focus on living

118

in and enjoying the present with an attitude of gratitude for the chance to be alive.

"By accepting your limits and choosing beliefs that help you deal with the unknowable, you can feel a sense of purpose and inner peace.

- "Educate your mind. Improve your ability to cope with stress by reading about human growth, stress, and the dimensions of life; arm yourself with knowledge."

D. Improving Your Physical Condition

- "Do regular physical exercise. Inactivity is a serious health hazard. Regular, vigorous exercise (especially aerobic exercises that have cardiovascular benefits) reduces anxiety, inhibits unwarranted mental and physical behavior, and produces a fatigued state that further reduces such behavior. In other words, the attention that has to be focused on vigorous activities (tennis, jogging, etc.) counteracts mental and physical anxiety. Physical exercise is also a way to work off stress by relieving tension. This makes it easier to handle problems more calmly. Each of us needs a safety-valve activity or outlet for pent-up emotions. Activities that are good for high mental and physical stress include running, brisk walking, swimming, biking, active sports, and Hatha Yoga.

- "Develop a nutritionally balanced diet. We need to feed our bodies the right building and nourishment materials. Attention to proper nutrition is a form of insurance against disease and debilitation. Author Donald Ardell says, 'A major diet-related health hazard in our country is a combination of over-consumption and under-nutrition.'[1]

"There is much controversy about nutritional requirements these days. You need to study nutrition and then map out your own course. Some basics that are fairly widely accepted include:

  —cutting down on caffeine products: coffee, tea, cola
  —adding bran for bulk
  —reducing sugar intake
  —eating more raw fruits and vegetables
  —eating more unprocessed foods
  —supplementing your diet with vitamins and minerals
  —starting each day with a full breakfast

---

[1] Donald B. Ardell. *High Level Wellness: An Alternative to Doctors, Drugs and Disease.* Emmaus, Penn.: Rodale Press, 1977.

- "Relax. Be kind to yourself. Develop a quieting skill to reduce the effects of excessive sympathetic nervous activity. Design your week to include relaxing activities as a regular part of your life. Enjoy what you do to relax.

"Remember: anxiety and tension are incompatible with relaxation.

"Steps to relax:
  - Become aware that you are tense; discriminate your level of tension.
  - Keep a record of tension and realize that you are responsible for excessive tension.
  - Incorporate relaxation into your daily life. Let go of tension voluntarily, either through activity or passively by lying down and going limp (D.M.R., autogenics, etc.)."

XI. SUMMING UP AND EVALUATION OF WORKSHOP

Summing Up
"Today we have given you a basic introduction to stress and stress management techniques that you can use to live a more healthy life."

Evaluation of Workshop
Hand out cards or paper for the evaluation.

"We have enjoyed working with you today and hope you will join us for other workshops. We would like some feedback from you on how you would evaluate the experience and would like you to answer the following questions:

- What is your assessment of the workshop? Are there ways it could be improved?
- How would you comment on the style and effectiveness of the leaders?
- What did you learn about yourself and others today."

Ask participants to turn in evaluations. You may want to announce any upcoming groups or workshops and pass out handouts for participants to take home.

HANDOUTS FOR

STRESS MANAGEMENT

HOW MUCH STRESS IS IN YOUR LIFE?[1]

Dr. Thomas H. Holmes, a pioneering researcher in the field of stress-related illnesses at the University of Washington in Seattle, has designed a written test developed to predict your chances of getting sick in the near future in relation to the amount of stress in your life.

Score yourself on his Life Change Test. Check only those events which you have experienced in the past year.

Item No.	Item value	Happened ( )	Your Score	Life Event
1	100			Death of spouse
2	73			Divorce
3	65			Marital separation
4	63			Jail term
5	63			Death of close family member
6	53			Personal injury or illness
7	50			Marriage
8	47			Fired at work
9	45			Marital reconciliation
10	45			Retirement
11	44			Change in health of family member
12	40			Pregnancy
13	39			Sex difficulties
14	39			Gain of new family member
15	39			Business readjustment
16	38			Change in financial status
17	37			Death of close friend
18	36			Change to different line of work
19	35			Change in number of arguments with spouse
20	31			Mortgage over $10,000
21	30			Foreclosure of mortgage or loan

---

[1] T.H.Holmes and R.H.Rahe, "Social Readjustment Rating Scale." *Journal of Psychosomatic Research,* 11: 213: 1967. Oxford: United Kingdom: Pergamon Press. Used with permission of the publisher.

22	29	_____	_____	Change in responsibilities at work
23	29	_____	_____	Son or daughter leaving home
24	29	_____	_____	Trouble with in-laws
25	28	_____	_____	Outstanding personal achievement
26	26	_____	_____	Wife begins or stops work
27	26	_____	_____	Begin or end school
28	25	_____	_____	Change in living conditions
29	24	_____	_____	Revision of personal habits
30	23	_____	_____	Trouble with boss
31	20	_____	_____	Change in work hours or conditions
32	20	_____	_____	Change in residence
33	20	_____	_____	Change in schools
34	19	_____	_____	Change in recreation
35	19	_____	_____	Change in church activities
36	18	_____	_____	Change in social activities
37	17	_____	_____	Mortgage or loan less than $10,000
38	16	_____	_____	Change in sleeping habits
39	15	_____	_____	Change in number of family get-togethers
40	15	_____	_____	Change in eating habits
41	13	_____	_____	Vacation
42	12	_____	_____	Christmas
43	11	_____	_____	Minor violations of the law

Total score for 12 months _____

According to Dr. Holmes, the more change you have, the more likely you are to get sick. Of those who scored over 300 "life-change units," 80 percent get sick in the near future. With 150-299 life-change units, about 50 percent get sick in the near future. With less than 150 life-change units, about 30 percent get sick in the near future.

SELF-OBSERVABLE SIGNS OF STRESS[1]

_____ 1. General irritability, hyperexcitation, or depression

_____ 2. Pounding of the heart, an indicator of high blood pressure.

_____ 3. Dryness of the throat and mouth.

_____ 4. Impulsive behavior, emotional instability.

_____ 5. The overpowering urge to cry or run and hide.

_____ 6. Inability to concentrate, flight of thoughts and general disorientation.

_____ 7. Feelings of unreality, weakness, or dizziness.

_____ 8. Predilection to become fatigued, and loss of "joie de vivre."

_____ 9. "Floating anxiety," that is to say, we are afraid although we do not know exactly what we are afraid of.

_____ 10. Emotional tension and alertness, feeling of being "keyed up."

_____ 11. Trembling, nervous tics.

_____ 12. Tendency to be easily startled by small sounds, etc.

_____ 13. High-pitched nervous laughter.

_____ 14. Stuttering and other speech difficulties.

_____ 15. Bruxism, or grinding of the teeth.

_____ 16. Insomnia.

_____ 17. Hypermotility. This is technically called "hyperkinesia," an increased tendency to move about without any reason, an inability to just take a physically relaxed attitude, sitting quietly in a chair or lying on a sofa.

_____ 18. Sweating.

_____ 19. The frequent need to urinate.

---

[1] From *The Stress of Life* by Dr. Hans Selye, pp. 174-177. Copyright 1978 by McGraw-Hill Book Company. Used with permission of the publisher.

_____ 20. Diarrhea, indigestion, queasiness in the stomach, and sometimes even vomiting.

_____ 21. Migraine headaches.

_____ 22. Premenstrual tension or missed menstrual cycles.

_____ 23. Pain in the neck or lower back.

_____ 24. Loss of or excessive appetite.

_____ 25. Increased smoking.

_____ 26. Increased use of legally prescribed drugs, such as tranquilizers or amphetamines.

_____ 27. Alcohol and drug addiction.

_____ 28. Nightmares.

_____ 29. Neurotic behavior.

_____ 30. Psychoses.

_____ 31. Accident proneness.

TYPES OF STRESS AND SUGGESTED RELAXATION TECHNIQUES FOR EACH

PHYSICAL: Bodily or Somatic Stress

Deep Muscle Relaxation
Progressive Relaxation
Autogenic Training
Meditation on Bodily Focus (i.e., breathing)
Hatha Yoga
Massage
Deep Breathing Exercises
Exercise

MENTAL: Cognitive Stress

Meditation (Relaxation Response Format)
Hatha Yoga
Deep Breathing with Visualization
Progressive Relaxation with Cognitive Focus and Visualization
Active Generation of Cognitive Behavior (playing chess, etc.)
Involvement of Entire Perceptual-Cognitive System (Watching TV or a
    movie, reading)
Activities (dancing, walking, sports)
Systematic Desensitization
Hypnosis

COMBINATION OF PHYSICAL AND MENTAL STRESS

Vigorous Physical Exercise—e.g., jogging, running, biking, hiking, swim-
    ming, tennis, martial art forms, basketball, volleyball, etc.; attention-
    ally demanding physically or mentally.

SUMMARY OF DEEP MUSCLE RELAXATION TECHNIQUE

You can learn to relax all large muscle groups in your body. The method requires that you *tense* (tighten up and hold the tension) and then *relax* the muscle. Each time you do this, *concentrate* on the difference in body sensations and feelings between the tension and relaxation. Learning these feelings will help you become aware of any tense muscles which you can then relax. The exercise progresses as follows:

Right hand and forearm—2 times

Left hand and forearm—2 times

Biceps—bend elbow—once

Triceps—arms stretched out—once

Forehead—wrinkle up—once

Forehead—wrinkle down—once

Eyes—close tightly—once

Tongue—pressed up to roof of mouth—once

Neck—head pressed back—once

Neck—head pressed back, rolling head to the left and to the right—
    2 times

Shoulders—shrugged up—2 times

Chest—deep breath, hold it, exhale slowly—2 times

Stomach—hold it in—2 times

Stomach—hold it out—2 times

Lower back—arch it up—2 times

Thighs—press down on heels—2 times

Calves—toes forward—2 times

Shins—toes up and back—2 times

Try to practice this exercise two times daily to build up a habit of relaxation.

SUMMARY OF RELAXATION RESPONSE TECHNIQUE, Developed by Dr. Herbert Benson, Harvard University.

The basic technique for the elicitation of the relaxation response is extremely simple. Its elements have been known and used for centuries in many cultures throughout the world.

Four basic elements are common to all these practices: a quiet environment, a mental device, a passive attitude, and a comfortable position. A simple, mental, noncultic technique based on these four elements follows.

1. **A quiet environment**
   One should choose a quiet, calm environment with as few distractions as possible. Sound, even background noise, may prevent the elicitation of the response. Choose a convenient, suitable place—for example, at an office desk in a quiet room.

2. **A mental device**
   The meditator employs the constant stimulus of a single-syllable sound or word. The syllable is repeated silently or in a low, gentle tone. The purpose of the repetition is to free oneself from logical, externally oriented thought by focusing solely on the stimulus. Many different words and sounds have been used in traditional practices. Because of its simplicity and neutrality, the use of the syllable "one" is suggested.

3. **A passive attitude**
   The purpose of the response is to help one rest and relax, and this requires a completely passive attitude. One should not scrutinize his or her performance or try to force the response, because this may well prevent the response from occurring. When distracting thoughts enter the mind, they should simply be disregarded.

4. **A comfortable position**
   The meditator should sit in a comfortable chair in as restful a position as possible. The purpose is to reduce muscular effort to a minimum. The head may be supported; the arms should be balanced or supported as well. The shoes may be removed and the feet propped up several inches, if desired. Loosen all tight-fitting clothing.

Eliciting the Relaxation Response
Using these four basic elements, one can evoke the response by following
this simple, mental, noncultic procedure:

1. In a quiet environment, sit in a comfortable position.

2. Close your eyes.

3. Deeply relax your muscles, beginning at your feet and progressing up
   to your face—feet, calves, thighs, lower torso, chest, shoulders, neck,
   head.
   Allow them to remain deeply relaxed.

4. Breathe through your nose. Become aware of your breathing. As you
   breathe out, say the word "one" silently to yourself. Thus: breathe
   in. . . breathe out, with "one." In. . . out, with "one". . .

5. Continue this practice for 20 minutes. You may open your eyes to
   check the time, but do not use an alarm. When you finish, sit quietly
   for several minutes, at first with your eyes closed and later with your
   eyes open.

Remember not to worry about whether you are successful in achieving a
deep level of relaxation—maintain a passive attitude and permit relaxation
to occur at its own pace. When distracting thoughts occur, ignore them
and continue to repeat "one" as you breathe. The technique should be
practiced once or twice daily, and not within two hours after any meal,
since the digestive processes seem to interfere with the elicitation of the
expected changes.

STRESS MANAGEMENT TECHNIQUES AND PRINCIPLES

A. Managing Your Time and Energy

Self-Assessment

- Listen to your body and your feelings for signals of stress.

- Evaluate your present habits. What price do you pay in terms of stress, discomfort, or lack of enjoyment in life?

- Be aware of high-stress habits: speaking fast, competing constantly, ignoring or denying tiredness, setting quotas, doing two things at once, pretending to listen, overscheduling, clenching your fists or jaws.

- Look for stressors—people, places, things—and take responsibility for trying to lower your stress.

- Find your stress quotient. Ask yourself, Am I taking on too much? If so, slow down your life and your drive.

Planning and Setting Goals

- Set priorities: choose how to spend your time and energy to balance your life, control your tempo, achieve a healthy balance between work and play, and develop commitment.

- Schedule time for recreation and hobbies: try to maximize your enjoyment of life. The noise and rush of modern life may keep us in a constantly stimulated state and contribute to a feeling of anxiety. Take a breather, relax, allow yourself time to get places. Take time to enjoy the trip and time to reflect.

B. Improving Your Environment

- Reduce unnecessary noises and irritations.

- Get enough rest and sleep in order to be alert and able to cope with stress.

- Don't use passive, habit-forming ways to blot out stress symptoms— drugs or alcohol—which later cause more stress. These make you dependent on means outside of yourself for control of stress.

- Anticipate changes and crises; plan how you will deal with stresses— a promotion, a disappointment, for example. Remember that the ability to handle stress comes from within.

- Improve the way you relate to others. Learn to be more open and honest and to express your feelings and share yourself with others. (Assertiveness training can help here.) Learn to express anger constructively.

- Build a support system: find security, develop new friendships, ask friends for extra strokes when you need them. Be more open with people, don't criticize or blame others, give in occasionally, do something for others, get involved.

- Build a comfortable home atmosphere: change your residence, redecorate, put yourself into your physical surroundings and create a comfortable scene around you.

C. Improving Your Internal Environment

- Develop a positive attitude toward life. Put stressors in a favorable context. If you can convince yourself that some of the stress is useful or necessary, you will reduce the aftereffects of stress. In other words, recognize the beneficial aspects of stress, even to the point of seeking growth lessons in bad experiences. Use the power of positive thinking; your attitude determines whether you perceive any experience as pleasant or unpleasant. People actually control how they choose to see things. Marcus Aurelius said, "If you are distressed by anything external, the pain is not due to the thing itself but to your estimate of it. This you have the power to revoke at any time."

- Learn to take it easy. Many of us take things too seriously and need to take one thing at a time. When we worry too much we need diversion—something to put in the place of worrying—a pleasant thought, thought stoppage (a technique to stop negative thought patterns by shouting words like "stop" or "no" in the middle of an anxious series of thoughts), or change of scene (getting away from a painful situation in order to catch your breath and give yourself a new perspective—going to a movie, reading, visiting a friend—doing something to escape from your routine). Remember, "Worry is like rocking in a rocking chair. It gives you something to do, but gets you nowhere" (unknown author).

- Set aside quieting time. Practice the relaxation response or deep muscle relaxation. Regulating the activity of your mind or body will reduce unwanted activity in that mode. Practicing meditation with visualization helps reduce worrying and anxious thoughts and D.M.R. helps reduce tension in the body.

132

• Talk out your worries with a friend or a professional (if preoccupied with emotional problems). This helps clarify problems and control anxiety. Therapy, by helping you relax and become aware of your feelings and behavior, helps you remain calm in otherwise anxious situations.

• Set your goals on inner peace and serenity. We all need to learn to accept what we cannot change, to learn to love ourselves, and not to be afraid. Instead of worrying about the past or the future, focus on living in and enjoying the present with an attitude of gratitude for the chance to be alive.

By accepting your limits and choosing beliefs that help you deal with the unknowable, you can feel a sense of purpose and inner peace.

• Educate your mind. Improve your ability to cope with stress by reading about human growth, stress, and the dimensions of life; arm yourself with knowledge.

D. Improving Your Physical Condition

• Do regular physical exercise. Inactivity is a serious health hazard. Regular, vigorous exercise (especially aerobic exercises that have cardiovascular benefits) reduces anxiety, inhibits unwarranted mental and physical behavior, and produces a fatigued state that further reduces such behavior. In other words, the attention that has to be focused on vigorous activities (tennis, jogging, etc.) counteracts mental and physical anxiety. Physical exercise is also a way to work off stress by relieving tension. This makes it easier to handle problems more calmly. Each of us needs a safety-valve activity or outlet for pent-up emotions. Activities that are good for high mental and physical stress include running, brisk walking, swimming, biking, active sports, and Hatha Yoga.

• Develop a nutritionally balanced diet. We need to feed our bodies the right building and nourishment materials. Attention to proper nutrition is a form of insurance against disease and debilitation. Author Donald Ardell says, "A major diet-related health hazard in our country is a combination of over-consumption and under-nutrition."[1]

---

[1] Donald B. Ardell. *High Level Wellness: An Alternative to Doctors, Drugs and Disease.* Emmaus, Penn.: Rodale Press, 1977.

There is much controversy about nutritional requirements these days. You need to study nutrition and then map out your own course. Some basics that are fairly widely accepted include:

—cutting down on caffeine products: coffee, tea, cola
—adding bran for bulk
—reducing sugar intake
—eating more raw fruits and vegetables
—eating more unprocessed foods
—supplementing your diet with vitamins and minerals
—starting each day with a full breakfast

• Relax. Be kind to yourself. Develop a quieting skill to reduce the effects of excessive sympathetic nervous activity. Design your week to include relaxing activities as a regular part of your life. Enjoy what you do to relax.

Remember: anxiety and tension are incompatible with relaxation.

Steps to relax:

—Become aware that you are tense; discriminate your level of tension.

—Keep a record of tension and realize that you are responsible for excessive tension.

—Incorporate relaxation into your daily life. Let go of tension voluntarily, either through activity or passively by lying down and going limp (D.M.R., autogenics, etc.).